WHEN IT ALL BREAKS BAD

TEN THINGS TO DO (AND NOT DO) AFTER
BETRAYAL

MICHELLE D. MAYS, LPC, CSAT-S

RELATIONAL RECOVERY PRESS

Editing by Scott Brassart Graphic design by Sandy Flewelling / TrueBlue Design Cover Photography: Kevin Carden/AdobeStock

CONTENTS

FOREWORD

Just a few words about me and this book before we get started so you won't feel lost when I refer to certain things...

I'm a Licensed Professional Counselor and have been in the psychotherapy field for over 17 years, specializing in betrayal trauma, sexual addiction, childhood trauma, and relationship issues. I came to the work of treating sex addiction and betrayal trauma partially through my own story of being married to a sex addict for many years. I went through the crisis of betrayal, the resulting trauma, and a recovery process that changed my life. At times throughout this book I will refer to parts of my own story.

In 2011, after a decade in private practice, I founded the Center for Relational Recovery (CRR). CRR is grounded in the belief that all significant life changes happen in the context of relationships, and our attachments to others are therefore the most meaningful and at times the most challenging parts of our lives. CRR offers an outpatient treatment program that simultaneously treats the cheating/addicted partner, the betrayed partner, and the relationship. You will hear me refer to my work with clients at CRR throughout this book.

I'm also the founder of PartnerHope.com, an online resource offering authentic hope to betrayed partners. I blog there each week

on the topic of betrayal trauma. The site also offers free download-
able resources that you may find helpful. PartnerHope.com is steadily
developing into a more robust resource. If you want to stay connected
to what is coming up, you can go to PartnerHope.com and subscribe
to the blog.

It is always a dilemma, when writing about intimate betrayal, to
determine who to write to. Language is limiting and the constant
insertion of he/she, him/her, herself/himself, etc., makes for cumber-
some reading. For the sake of readability, I have used the pronouns
she/her when talking about the betrayed partner and the pronouns
he/him when talking about the cheating partner. If this categoriza-
tion does not apply to you, I hope that you will be able to overlook it,
changing the pronouns in your mind and reading the book as it
applies to you and your situation. In my experience, whether you are
male or female or somewhere in between and you have faced
betrayal, the information in this book is relevant.

Regarding the description of relationship betrayal and the role of
the cheating partner, I have interchangeably used the terms cheating,
cheater, infidelity, and unfaithfulness. I have used these terms
descriptively and not with any intent of pejorative labeling of the
individual who is in this position in the relationship.

I have also talked both about sexual betrayal that results from
being in a relationship with a sex addict and sexual betrayal that
results from 'old fashioned' cheating without an addiction or compulsivity component. I do this because, for betrayed partners, the experience of betrayal trauma is very similar regardless of the where the
cheating originates. So whether I am using examples involving
sexual addiction or standard infidelity, the information will likely be
on point for you.

Lastly, I would like to state that some betrayed partners who are
reading this book are going to decide to stay in their relationship and
work toward healing. They will decide they love their partner and
they want to see if all that they and their partner have invested in the
relationship can be salvaged. And their cheating partner may be truly
repentant and willing to do whatever he has to do to heal the damage

wrought by his behaviors. Other betrayed partners are going to decide that they need to leave their relationship in order to heal. (There is a whole chapter in this book to help you think about that big decision.)

Whatever you decide for yourself and your relationship, the contents of this book will fit your situation. I have tucked information throughout the book that applies to the specific circumstances of each of these choices. For the most part, however, the material is useful regardless of your decision to stay or leave.

INTRODUCTION

When you discover that your partner has cheated on you, shock waves reverberate through your heart. Everything dear about your significant other – his face, voice, feel, and smell – has been transformed from that which is familiar, comforting, and safe into a treacherous, untrustworthy stranger.

Cheating is unveiled in countless ways. Sometimes the practical unromantic details of everyday living reveal the secret double life. A condom is found in a pocket, a text is not deleted, a revealing charge shows up on the cheater's credit card, an illicit conversation is overheard, a hotel calls about a lost item, an internet history provides evidence. Other times, cheating is exposed through a cataclysm of drama. The affair partner's spouse calls. A routine medical visit becomes anything but. There is an arrest. There is no longer any money in the retirement account. A prestigious job is lost. The story is on the news.

As if the variety of ways discovery unfolds is not enough, cheating itself comes in the largest crayon box imaginable, filled with every hue and color of emotional and sexual betrayal. There are anonymous sex-based encounters, long-term emotional and sexual affairs, sex that is paid for, sex that is traded for, emotional entanglements, texting and sexting, online hookups, sex that violates boundaries, sex that is compulsive, sex that is addictive, and porn, porn, and more porn.

For the one who is cheated on, no matter how it is revealed, no matter the details of who, what, when, where, and how, and regardless of whether the betrayal arises from old-fashioned infidelity or a sexual addiction run rampant, the essential and most painful facet of the cheating always comes down to the wound of being lied to, manipulated, and having one's trust betrayed.

Sexual betrayal is an earthquake that convulses the foundation of your relationship. And it is followed by a tsunami of consequences, repercussions, outcomes, emotions, and reactions. For the betrayed partner, there is shock, fear, and an overwhelming sense of bewilderment. What is happening? Why? What do I do? How will I survive this? Will *we* survive this?

During this initial period of overwhelm, when the body is experiencing the traumatic impact of being betrayed, the mind struggles for a sense of clarity and direction. There is confusion, disorientation, and reality fragmentation as the world you knew comes apart and then stitches itself back together in a strange and unwelcome shape.

This is a time when help is needed: a sense of direction, a light pointing the way, some kind of marker to show you where to step next. And that is what this book is for. This book is written to help you regain your footing and walk forward once again.

Here is the good news about betrayal: others have experienced it too. Countless people have felt the earthquake, survived the tsunami, and rebuilt lives filled with meaning, purpose, and joy. Because of this, there is shared wisdom and guidance to draw on, especially during the first uncertain days after betrayal's discovery.

This book is born out of the collective insight, discernment, and experience of betrayed partners who have walked through the fire and come out the other side. I asked a group of betrayed partners to tell me the ten most important things that they needed to know and to do in the aftermath of betrayal, and the ten most important things to not do. I received shockingly similar lists. Over and over, the same things were expressed. The responses I got were written differently and highlighted a variety of circumstances, but the core issues were the same.

This book is my attempt to flesh out what these betrayed partners shared with me and to provide a starting point for you as you begin the process of healing from betrayal. The book is laid out in ten chapters with each chapter discussing a key element of healing – something 'to do' in the early stages of healing. Each chapter also contains a related 'what not to do' discussion covering the pitfalls and detours that betrayed partners sometimes stumble into. If you can avoid doing these things, your journey will go faster and more smoothly.

As you read the book, feel free to take it in order or to skip around, selecting the chapters that feel most relevant for you in the moment. However you decide to utilize this resource, I suggest that you take it slowly, giving yourself plenty of space and time to process what you are reading. Pay attention to the feelings that come up and allow them to be felt and processed. Be kind to yourself. Be patient and trust that you are indeed going to heal and you will once again be whole.

1

TO DO: GET EXPERT HELP

Regardless of whether you are thinking about staying in or leaving your relationship, getting guidance and support from someone trained in dealing with betrayal trauma is one of the best things you can do to help yourself.

For most betrayed partners, getting help is a high priority. However, the emphasis is typically on finding a therapist for your significant other or for the two of you as a couple. Partners often place themselves last in line for getting quality help and support. In my experience, however, the individuals and couples who do the best in terms of healing and recovery are those who combine individual therapy for *both* partners with couple's therapy.

You as an individual need help and support from someone trained in treating betrayal trauma. You have been deeply impacted by what has taken place. Trauma is an experience that hijacks your brain and body, putting you into a fear state and changing the way you function. You need someone skilled in treating trauma, a professional who understands the neurobiology of your experience and can skillfully work with you to intervene and resolve your trauma symptoms. Having a safe place that is just yours, where you can sort through your confusing, chaotic thoughts and feelings, is essential to your personal process of healing.

If you are hoping to heal your relationship, individual therapy will also help with that. In couple's therapy, you are not the client, and neither is your partner. The client is your relationship. When each of you has a place to process through the individual issues that are coming up, it allows the couple's therapist to focus on your relationship. Couple's therapy does not have to divert from its primary purpose to manage the individual issues that might complicate and slow things down. Instead, couple's work can stay focused on the relationship and helping you and your partner heal and repair your bond with one another.

Finding the Right Help

In the aftermath of betrayal, finding help is a priority, but finding the *right* help is the key to things improving quickly. For example, therapy for those dealing with sexual addiction follows a very different course than therapy for those dealing with infidelity without a compulsivity component. As such, it is important that the therapist you work with is able to do what we call "differential diagnosis," accurately determining what type of problem you are dealing with and what the best treatment for that problem is.

Recently, my clinical team and I began working with a couple dealing with addiction. The husband had been using alcohol, cocaine, and sex compulsively. As we unwrapped the layers surrounding his behaviors, his addiction to alcohol and drugs was obvious. We also found that when he was drinking and using, he acted out sexually. But when he was not drinking and using, he was not compulsive with sex. The wife was sure he was a sex addict and needed sex addiction treatment. And of course, her biggest wounds were around the sexual betrayal, so she wanted assurance that he would be treated for that and those behaviors would stop.

However, the reality is that he is not a sex addict. He has alcohol and drug-induced sexual behavior. He needs substance abuse treatment plus couple's therapy to repair the damage done in the relation-ship, but he does not need sex addiction treatment.

If you have a therapist who is not well versed and trained in the different forms of betrayal and the ways that betrayal might manifest, you may end up with a misdiagnosis and the wrong type of treatment.

Individual Therapy for Betrayal Trauma

The very first thing that *you* need is a therapist for you personally who understands the complex dynamics of intimate betrayal, knows how to effectively treat betrayal trauma, and, if you are the partner of a sex addict, thoroughly understands sex addiction and the dynamics that couples dealing with sexual addiction typically experience.

Allow me, for just a moment, to step up onto my soapbox about this. I see many general practitioner therapists who believe they are equipped to treat betrayed partners. They do not see this population as one that requires specialized treatment. Instead, they view these issues through a more generalized lens. As a result, when betrayed partners come into their practice, they keep them as clients and work with them – often to the detriment of the client and the client's rela-tionship.

I have been working with betrayal trauma, sexual addiction, and infidelity for 17 years and I am still learning every day how to increase the effectiveness of my work. With betrayal trauma, there are unique and specific dynamics that individuals and couples are facing. If you are dealing with intimate betrayal, you need more than a generalized practitioner. You need someone trained in working with infidelity and/or sexual addiction, trained in working with attachment injuries in couples' relationships, and trained in working with relational trauma.

When I was married to my sexually addicted husband, I spent years trying to find help with general practitioners who, though well-meaning, did not help and in some cases made things significantly worse. What changed things for me was that when I entered graduate school and hit my bottom in terms of my own unhealthy coping behaviors, I went to the president of my school and said, "I need a referral to a therapist, but I don't want to see someone who says they treat addiction. I need a specialist who works with the partners of addicts. I need to see someone who knows what they are doing and specifically works with people in my situation. Do you have a recommendation?" Thankfully, he had a great recommendation, and I started seeing a therapist who understood the dynamics I was caught in and set me on the path to healing.

That was a turning point for me in every way. As soon as I had good help and support behind me, solid direction and wisdom to guide me, my life began to change. I began to experience healing and transformation in my life in ways that stunned me and filled me with joy. So I tell you from personal experience: Never underestimate the power of skilled, knowledgeable help.

So how do you find this type of help? One place to look, even if you are not dealing with sexual addiction, is for a Certified Sexual Addiction Therapist (CSAT). These therapists specialize in working with individuals and clients whose lives are in high distress thanks to compulsive cheating. They receive a great deal of training in working with betrayed partners and betrayal trauma. You can find a directory of CSAT therapists at www.sexhelp.com.

Another place to look is with The Association of Partners of Sex Addicts Trauma Specialists (APSATS). This organization certifies individuals in working with betrayed partners. They have both licensed therapists and coaches available to offer support. You can find APSATS certified counselors and coaches at **www.apsats.org**.

Lastly, you can look for Marriage and Family Therapists (MFTs) who specialize in treating infidelity and work with both couples and individuals. Looking through the therapist directories that I mention below in the couple's therapy section is a good place to start with this.

Couple's Therapy for Infidelity

If you are dealing with infidelity without sexual addiction, you will want to look for a couple's therapist who understands the dynamics of infidelity and how to help couples heal the wounds (the 'attachment injuries') that have damaged the relational bond. You will want a couple's therapist trained in approaches that specifically address the repair of ruptured bonds, the restoration of emotional safety, and learning how to deeply connect with one another emotionally.

You will also want a therapist who understands how to work with a cheating partner who is not yet ready to tell the whole truth about his history of cheating or is still involved in the cheating behavior. This creates a complicated dynamic in couple's therapy, and it is important that the therapist not assume that full disclosure has occurred and you're ready to move toward vulnerability and repair. That work should not occur before full disclosure of the depth and scope of the betrayal has taken place.

Therapists trained in Emotionally Focused Therapy for Couples (EFT) are particularly skilled with these issues. The International Centre for Excellence in Emotionally Focused Therapy has a therapist directory at http://iceeft.com/find-a-therapist that will help you locate a certified EFT specialist in your area. Another option is to look for someone trained in working with betrayal trauma by the Gottman Institute, www.gottman.com/couples/private-therapy, which specializes in research-based approaches to helping couples dealing with betrayal. If you know other people who have dealt with issues like your own, you may want to ask them where they found useful help. If you're in a 12-step recovery program, asking others in the group where they found support can also be helpful.

Couple's Therapy for Sex Addiction

If you are in a relationship with a sex addict – a person with an ongoing pattern of compulsive sexual behavior – you will want to find a therapist trained and credentialed in treating sexual addiction. Be wary of therapists who claim to treat sexual addiction even though they have not received any formal training or certification.

You should also steer clear of therapists who believe that sex addicts need specialized help but their betrayed partners can be treated by a general practitioner. This approach ignores the level of traumatic injury experienced by the partner and underestimates the level of skill needed to intervene effectively. It also ignores the specific and unique challenges that couples dealing with sexual addiction face, including the timing and pacing of the therapy needed to manage those unique issues effectively.

One place to look for skilled help is the International Institute of Trauma and Addiction Professionals, https://www.iitap.com/. This organization trains and certifies sex addiction therapists (CSATs) and has a therapist directory that is searchable by location. Another option is the Society for the Advancement of Sexual Health at www.sash.net. They also have a searchable directory of therapists who specialize in treating problematic sexual behaviors.

What to Look For

When looking for a therapist, don't be afraid to interview the therapist and ask about his or her credentials and experience. If you can, visit more than one therapist to determine who is the best fit for you. Ask potential therapists to explain how they assess the problem and decide on the proper treatment path. Explore how they provide treatment, what training they have received, and what treatment models they use. Ask them to explain how they see your individual treatment interacting with your partner's treatment and treatment for you as a couple.

In addition, you will want to ask the therapist about how he or she will collaborate with other treatment professionals involved in your treatment. As stated earlier, you may have one therapist, your partner may have another therapist, and together you may have a couple's therapist. This is a lot of cooks in the kitchen, so it is vital that everyone communicates and coordinates treatment. Unfortunately, not all therapists are collaborative, so this is an important question to ask and to insist upon before choosing a therapist.

Without the coordinated efforts of the whole treatment team, one person can be working at cross-purposes to another without knowing it.

It Gets Better

Finding good help at the beginning of the process helps things get better quicker. It helps you to feel that you are not alone and that someone has the knowledge and expertise to walk you and your significant other through the healing process. When you and your partner get coordinated help, things stabilize more quickly, as everyone is on the same page, pulling in the same direction, with less conflict as you negotiate boundaries and establish safe zones in your relationship.

WHAT NOT TO DO: DECIDE YOU DON'T NEED HELP

For many betrayed partners it can feel unbelievable that in the aftermath of being cheated on, lied to, betrayed, and traumatized they are now being asked to go to therapy, attend a support group, or engage in a treatment program of some kind.

Here are some of the things I have had partners say to me:

"I didn't do anything wrong. Why do I have to go to therapy?"

"It's not fair that because of something he did I have to take my time and spend my money on treatment."

"Why should I work on our relationship when he clearly hasn't cared about it at all?"

These comments can be summed up into one big screaming protest of "IT'S NOT FAIR!"

And you know what? Betrayed partners are absolutely right. It's NOT fair. It's not even in the same county as fair. However, if you let the unfairness drive your decision making, that will create negative consequences for you.

I want you to imagine for a moment that someone you love very much, a best friend or a sister, has been hit by a school bus and is badly injured. When you show up at the hospital emergency room she is trying to check herself out in spite of the fact that her head is bleeding, her leg has a bone sticking out of it, and she can't move one of her arms.

You are astonished and ask them what in the bleep she is doing? She responds, "That stupid bus driver hit me with his bus. I wasn't doing anything wrong. I was minding my own business, staying in my lane, going the speed limit, and BAM! He hit me. I'm not staying here a single minute and spending my good money, time, and energy when it is not my fault and I didn't do anything wrong. It's not fair that he hit me and I'm going home!"

I'm guessing you would be very angry at that bus driver for hurting your loved one. But you would also be worried about her. You would want her to spend whatever time, money, and energy it took to be well again. You would even wonder what was wrong with her that she thought she didn't need help just because she didn't cause the problem. You would encourage her to get back on the gurney and let the doctors care for her. You might even offer to drive her to physical therapy, encouraging her to stick with it until she was fully operational and healed.

Betrayal trauma is a lot like getting hit by a bus. Regardless of not causing it, regardless of it not being your fault, you still got hit and you have been hurt. You didn't ask for it, yet it has happened to you anyway. And in spite of your best efforts to cope, it has impacted you and very likely traumatized you, creating a whole series of unasked for problems and consequences in your life. Just like your imaginary loved one above, you need help and support to heal.

My hope for you is that, despite being hit by the incredibly unfair bus crash of betrayal, you will do whatever you need to do to help yourself heal and come through the experience a stronger, wiser, more vibrant version of yourself. You are worth whatever time, energy, and money it takes to help you to cope with what has happened.

. . .

I'm Divorcing, So I Can Just Move On

Recently a client decided that the best and healthiest route for her was to end her relationship with her spouse. He had cheated on her and his demeanor after discovery was removed, distant, and often passive-aggressive. She came to therapy, told her counselor about her decision, and declared that she was done with treatment. Since she was divorcing, she no longer needed therapy.

Please don't do this.

When someone makes this type of decision I feel sad and worried for that person because the decision is so short-sighted. The belief that if you are divorcing the person who betrayed you, you no longer need help reflects the idea that your betrayer is the one and only problem and if you get rid of that person you will be fine. It ignores the bus crash of betrayal trauma that you have experienced, and the ways in which your relationship and the infidelity have impacted you.

Even worse, when you terminate therapy and don't work through what has happened in your relationship, giving yourself room to grieve its loss and to heal, you inevitably carry your unresolved baggage from that relationship into the next one. You then manifest your unresolved issues on your next partner, which is not healthy, not fair, and not the way to have a successful new relationship.

Many (probably most) betrayed partners are left with significant trust issues. They are wounded around their sexuality and sexual self-perception, as well as how they think about other people's sexuality. They feel unclear about what happened between them and their significant other. As a result, they are often limited in their ability to connect, be vulnerable, take risks, and be intimate in a healthy manner.

If time and attention are not given to working through the significant impact of relationship betrayal, these unresolved issues can and likely will affect your ability to choose a different type of partner next time and to be in a relationship in a different (healthier and more emotionally fulfilling) way.

I have worked with many betrayed partners who have a pattern of hitching their emotional wagons to unhealthy partners. Some of these clients have married sex addicts repeatedly. Others have experi-enced infidelity over and over. Still others pick addicts of different stripes – one time an alcoholic, next time a sex addict, then a drug addict, etc. Usually this is because the betrayed partner's personal history and family of origin dynamics leave that person blind to the red flags that others would see and run away from. Working through your relationship history and understanding the unconscious forces that guide who you pick and how you enter relationships is vital if you hope to select better partners and have better relationships in the future.

If you are leaving your relationship, please give yourself the gift of getting good help and taking the time to sort through what has happened, to grieve what you have lost, to heal the wounds caused by betrayal, and to learn how to enter your next relationship with your eyes wide open and the ability to deeply connect in a healthy way.

You are Worthy of Help and Support

No matter what has happened and no matter what will happen with your relationship, you have experienced a major life event that has changed you and changed your understanding of yourself and relationships. Giving yourself space, support, time, and energy to process this experience, grieve the losses that have occurred, learn more about who you are, and heal is vital for your future. You do not want to carry the wounds from the betrayal forward in your current relationship. You do not want to carry the wounds from this relation-ship into a future relationship. Giving yourself the gift of expert help is one of the most loving things you can do for yourself after experi-encing betrayal. I hope you will.

2

TO DO: REACH FOR A COMMUNITY OF SUPPORT

Managing the aftermath of betrayal is a relational task. You have experienced a relational trauma, and a relational problem requires a relational solution. This means you need a supportive community around you.

Before discovering betrayal, your primary relationship probably functioned as your 'safe base,' providing you with a felt sense of belonging, connection, and security. When relationships are functioning well, they provide this type of secure base, and this in turn provides a launching pad for the rest of life. The more secure you feel in your primary relationship, the more able you are to move into the world with confidence – to take risks and be your authentic self.

Betrayal trauma damages this sense of security. When you experience betrayal and your safe base is eroded, damaged, or disappears altogether, you suddenly find yourself in a state of free fall. Betrayal chips away at your sense of emotional, sexual, spiritual, and financial safety.

When we feel unsafe the primitive part of our brain lights up and sends us into survival mode. We run on adrenaline, cortisol, and other stress-induced chemicals and we do not function well. Instead of providing us with a launching pad, our relationship now feels like a source of danger and threat. We desperately scrabble around trying to find some piece of solid ground to stand on.

Finding Safe Friends for Support

To tolerate this type of uncertainty, not to mention the damage to your relationship, you need other people to fill in the gaps – to provide you with an alternative safe base for a while. You need a *community of support* that can walk with you and love you, providing helpful direction and care as you face the overwhelming emotions that come with deep betrayal.

I typically see betrayed partners do one of two things regarding finding people to bring into their inner circle.

On the one hand, they tell no one because they either are feeling such intense shame that it keeps them silent or they are afraid their friends and family will automatically judge them or their significant other. It feels easier to just soldier on alone than to take the risk of speaking to others about something so tender and painful.

On the other hand, they grab a bullhorn and broadcast to anyone who will listen all the gory details and secrets that they know, publicly shaming their significant other by airing every piece of dirty laundry as broadly as possible. This kind of boundary-less sharing is often an expression of anger and revenge toward the cheating partner for causing so much pain. It can also be an attempt to repudiate the shame that the betrayed partner may be feeling. Often, there is both shame about the betrayal and a niggling inner feeling that some lack in the betrayed partner has caused the infidelity. This can cause the betrayed partner to talk indiscriminately about her partner's behavior to try to prove to herself and others that it wasn't her fault and he is really the one to blame.

Neither isolating nor indiscriminately sharing the details with others is helpful. Instead, you want to thoughtfully and carefully look at your friends and family members, evaluate their suitability and availability, and select a few to invite into your inner circle. These are the folks to whom you will tell the details of what has happened – the people who will help you carry and work through your betrayal story.

How do you know who to invite into your inner circle? What makes someone a safe person? Happily, there are some easily identifiable qualities. Safe friends and family are those who:

- Respect and maintain your boundaries and do not gossip or share information that they have been entrusted with.
- Do not jump to conclusions about what you should do regarding your relationship, instead supporting your need to answer that question for yourself.
- Do not immediately turn against or judge your significant other, instead giving you the space and sounding board you need to work through your feelings, while encouraging you to maintain an open and gracious attitude toward your partner.
- Understand that you are in a process that takes time and are willing to be in that process with you, rather than rushing you toward "being done and moving on."
- Do not collude with you in pretending things are better than they are or deciding things are hopeless, instead holding a middle ground attitude and simply hearing your feelings as you bounce through the different emotions and reactions that betrayed partners typically have.
- Do not stoke your fear by telling you horror stories about things that have happened to other people or by joining you in imagining your worst-case scenarios.
- Have wisdom to share, and offer sound, thoughtful responses to the questions you ask.
- Are available and responsive when you need support.

Finding one or two people who are able and willing to provide this type of friendship and support can make all the difference. They give you a safe base to reach for and lean on when your primary relationship no longer provides this. They can hold your feelings with you, offer comfort, calm you down, and even join you in laughter. My hope is that you can find and reach out to at least one person who can walk with you in this way as you journey toward recovery. Because you are absolutely worthy of this attention, affirmation, and care.

Join a 12-Step Group

"You have *got* to be kidding me! You want me to go to a 12-step meeting when my partner is the cheater? What did I do to deserve that lovely suggestion? I'm not the problem. Why should I have to go to one of those meetings? I didn't do anything. And what if I see someone there that I know? I would just shrivel up and die if that happened. Plus, how is sitting in a room with a bunch of other people in my situation supposed to help me? And I've heard those meetings are either bitch sessions or they make it sound like *I'm* the problem because I'm codependent. Pigs will fly out of my you-know-what before I go to one of those meetings."

This colorful rant (in many equally vivid variations) is a relatively common response from betrayed partners when I first suggest that a 12-step meeting might be helpful. They tell me:

- I am not the problem, so why would I need a meeting?
- I resent having to spend my time and energy going to meetings when I haven't done anything wrong.
- They're just going to tell me that I'm the problem.
- It won't help.
- I'll see someone I know, and I'll be mortified.
- I don't want to be one of *those women*.
- Groups are fine for other people, but I don't need that.

I get it. No one wants to show up for a meeting where just by the simple act of being there you have identified yourself as a betrayed partner in a troubled relationship. No one wants to admit to that. Walking into a meeting where your mere presence suggests that you belong there and pretty much announces to the world that you are now one of *those women* can be incredibly difficult.

Many partners have talked to me about attending their first few meetings and feeling judgment and anger toward the other members. "Those women are pathetic, screwed up, weak, whiny, self-involved, pitiful, damaged, and no help whatsoever," they say. I assure these frustrated clients that they are experiencing a normal adjustment process, with their defense mechanisms of judgment and self-righteousness rising up to protect them from the painful realization that they, like the women they are judging, are reeling emotionally and struggling to find the best way forward. Eventually, they realize that they are a lot like those other women, even though they desperately do not want to be.

The clients who move through this phase and continue attending meetings typically find that as they get to know the other women, they start to hear the similarities rather than the differences. They start to understand who these women are and what they are dealing with – and they see themselves and their own lives in the process. A shift occurs, where self-compassion and compassion toward others increases, and the sense of isolation and of being "the only one" decreases. Friendships blossom and grow. Soon, the meeting becomes one of the key places to find support, useful advice, and empathy.

Often, when I first suggest 12-step meetings, my clients want to know how these meetings are supposed to help them. And that is a very good question, with a partly pragmatic, partly mysterious answer.

The pragmatic portion of the answer is that sitting in a room listening to and sharing with other people who have had your same experience causes the loneliness, isolation, and shame you feel to lift. Listening to each person in the room share and, at the end of the hour, realizing that you related to at least one thing that each person said even though you are all so very different from one another is a tremendous gift. Plus, you will hear ideas and nuggets of wisdom from those who are further down the road of healing, and this information can help you when similar situations arise in your own life. Finally, there is the wonderful experience of developing supportive friendships with others who understand exactly where you are and what you are feeling when the crap hits the fan.

The mysterious portion of the answer starts with the 12th step, which begins with the words, "Having had a spiritual awakening as the result of these steps..." There is something about working the 12 steps with a sponsor – a person who guides you through the process – that results in a spiritual transformation in your life. How and why this occurs is where the mystery comes in. But it does happen, and it affects every part of your life in a positive way. A deep inner transformation occurs, and you receive gifts that benefit you for the rest of your life.

Below is a list of 12-Step fellowships designed to help the partners and family members of addicts and cheaters:

- S-Anon (www.sanon.org) – for those in a relationship with a sex addict
- COSA (www.cosa-recovery.org) – for those in a relationship with a sex addict
- Adult Children of Alcoholics (www.adultchildren.org) – for anyone dealing with the effects of growing up in a dysfunctional family, not just for those who are children of alcoholics
- Al-Anon (www.al-anon.org) – for those in a relationship with an addict
- Recovery Couples Anonymous (www.recovering-couples.org) – for couples dealing with addiction
- Infidelity Survivors Anonymous (www.isurvivors.org) – for those dealing with infidelity; in-person meetings are only available in a few states

Join a Therapy Group

Not everyone will be in a location where therapy groups for betrayed partners are available. However, if you are so lucky, run don't walk and sign up to participate. I recently closed a women's therapy group for betrayed partners that I had been running for over 10 years. As I write this, I can see the faces of the women who came through that group, and I feel such love and admiration for all of them.

Group therapy of this type is where you will get some serious work done. It is where you learn to be intimate and vulnerable with others, allowing them to see your heart and revealing your most true self to them. You learn to take risks by using your voice to offer feedback or to ask the group for what you need. You learn to listen with different ears and to see through a different lens. You learn from watching others struggle and grow, and they in turn learn from your struggles and growth. Through this process, you end up forming some incredible bonds with the women you are in group with. Often, they become lifelong friends and integral parts of your ongoing inner circle of support.

Online Communities of Support

Not everyone lives in an area where trained therapists, group therapy, 12-step groups, or other resources are available. In such cases, the internet becomes an invaluable resource. There are a growing number of online communities and support services for betrayed partners. Some offer online courses, coaching appointments, eBooks, podcasts, and other material to guide you. Some also offer online support groups and forums where you can connect with other betrayed partners and learn from the experience, strength, and hope of those who have been where you are.

Intensive Workshops and Retreats

Another place to look for help and support is intensive workshops offered by treatment centers around the country specializing in addressing betrayal trauma. There are several three to eight-day intensives offered by well-respected experts in the field. These intensives can provide a place for you to go and focus solely on yourself and your needs. There is no going home at night and dealing with the kids or having to see your significant other at the end of the day. Instead, you have time to immerse yourself in your healing process, receiving education, help, and support in a surround sound environment.

Taking Care of You

The suggestions above are just some of the ways that you as a betrayed partner can find support, help, and care. The sooner you can get this in place, the sooner you will begin to heal and to feel a bit more stable. You need care, love, attention, support, and kindness right now. This is a time to let others give to you and to receive from them. There will be a time down the road when you give back, but right now is your time to be taken care of and supported.

WHAT NOT TO DO: ISOLATE

In the aftermath of betrayal, it can be tempting to isolate – curling into yourself and hiding from the rest of the world. When you are wounded, particularly in ways that create fear and a lack of emotional safety, an instinctual coping response is to distance yourself from others, hunkering down to privately nurse your hurting heart.

For the majority of betrayed partners, being cheated on creates feelings of shame. Questions arise such as:

- Am I good enough?
- Am I wanted?
- Do I matter?
- Am I worthy of loyalty and fidelity?
- Am I loveable?

- What does she (the acting out partner) have that I don't?
- Can I ever be enough?

These questions come from the shame that intimate betrayal so often leaves in its wake.

These feelings of shame, these feelings of being worthless and not good enough, make us want to hide. We do not want others to see our shame. The questions we have about whether we are truly valued by our partner (who just cheated on us) can spread out, impacting not just our primary relationship but all of our relationships. Suddenly we feel worthless with everyone, and this makes us want to turn away, cast our eyes toward the ground, and pull back into ourselves.

In the face of the feelings of rejection that being cheated on can bring, being vulnerable with other people – even in small ways – feels impossible. Isolating feels safer. Our need to create safety for ourselves in the middle of the profound fear we are experiencing can cause us to retreat from relationships both with our partner and with friends and family who may be wanting or available to support us.

While this is a normal coping response to betrayal shame, giving in to the pull of isolation actually heightens the shame, or, at a minimum, freezes it in place. It is in safe, supportive, caring connection with others that we have experiences that counter the shame that betrayal brings. When we feel heard, paid attention to, important, and as if we matter to those who reach out to care for us, that goes a long way toward countering the song of worthlessness that shame whispers in our ears.

When we isolate, our fear grows. Our minds, often stuck in a hyper-aroused state of fear and vigilance, imagine and prepare for the worst. We start to rehearse scripts of catastrophe and even larger rejections than what we have already experienced. Our fear can make the monster of infidelity grow and bloom into an Incredible Hulk of betrayal that devastates us over and over as our minds unspool one 'what if' scenario after another.

Staying connected to others keeps us grounded in reality. It soothes our threatened brains and helps us stay out of imagining even worse possibilities. Our relationships with safe friends, family members, and other support people give us places to talk about our fears, our sadness, our grief and loss. And in sharing those deeper emotions, we feel the relief of having them heard and held gently by those who care for us.

While the instinct toward isolation is understandable, my hope is that when you feel it, you will acknowledge the desire to pull in and protect yourself and then you will gently and kindly nudge yourself to instead reach out and be connected. For it is connection with others that allows our sense of safety to bloom and grow.

3

TO DO: EDUCATE YOURSELF

The next thing you are going to want to do is educate yourself about what has happened, what your options are, what recovery and healing involve and the steps in the process. And here is the good news: If you are reading this book, you have already started the process and are well on your way. Whether you are dealing with infidelity, sexual addiction or some other type of betrayal, there are resources available to help you understand both what is happening for your significant other and what is happening for you, and to help you feel empowered and equipped with information and support.

The list of podcasts, online courses, books, classes, webinars, and other resources for betrayed partners is growing as the need for help with betrayal trauma is more fully recognized. In addition to reading material, if you are near a counseling center specializing in treating betrayal trauma or sexual addiction you might also have access to educational workshops or therapy groups that can help you to get a more thorough understanding of the issues you are facing. Look around in your area, as you do not usually need to be a patient at the treatment center to participate in workshops or other educational events.

For recommendations of reading material, online resources, audio resources, and intensive treatment options, please visit www.-PartnerHope.com.

Rather than focus here on the many different types of educational resources that are available to you, I want to discuss how you engage in the process of gathering and processing information. *How* you enter this process is actually more important than *what* you take in.

Pace Yourself

Educating yourself about betrayal is just like everything else in the healing process: a marathon not a sprint. Nevertheless, many of the betrayed partners I treat tell me almost immediately that they have read everything there is to read about sexual addiction and partner trauma, and they know all there is to know about these topics.

I do believe that they have read a lot, but I do not believe that they know very much because almost 100 percent of the time they do not. Moreover, the partners who come in and have done tons of reading and searching for information are often in worse shape in terms of trauma symptoms than the partners who have sought out much less information. This probably seems counterintuitive, especially since I am suggesting that you want to spend time educating yourself. So, what gives here?

The reality is that you can only take in and truly absorb and understand a certain amount of new information in any given time-frame. If you flood yourself with book after book in one big rush, you get some head knowledge, but you don't get the experiential, whole-self learning where you truly absorb, chew on, and let the information change you.

Betrayed partners often feel so lost and unmoored that books and other resources provide an anchor. Books are a place to go to understand what is happening, to discover language that describes the experience, and to identify what to do next. It can be tempting to believe that if a little information is helpful, then more would be even better. But too much information means you aren't absorbing it and are unable to really use it.

You also need to understand that your headspace will be in different places as you walk the path of healing. So, information you read today will mean one thing, but a month from now it might mean something completely different. You will receive and process information differently at each step of the process. Sometimes it is helpful to have a preview of what is ahead, so you can keep the big picture in mind, but each step requires its own information, knowledge, and understanding, and it's impossible to just take the steps intellectually. You must experientially come to that part of the path and then learn how to walk it – and this best occurs slowly and deliberately.

So please pace yourself as you read, attend workshops, and engage in different ways of learning. Slower is actually faster in this situation. If you give yourself the time it really takes to chew on, absorb, experiment with, and internalize new information, skills, and tools, you will end up farther ahead in the end.

WHAT NOT TO DO: OVERWHELM YOURSELF

When I was in graduate school, we had to go on a day-long silent retreat. I was just beginning to understand that my spouse was dealing with sexual addiction, and I was trying to find material to read that might help me get my head around this fact. At that time, there were very few books for betrayed partners to choose from, but I finally found one. At the retreat, instead of meditating, journaling, or praying – all activities that would have been calming and grounding for me – I made the dubious decision to read this book about sex addiction. Oy.

I spent that retreat in a fit of screaming (albeit silent) terror. It's probably a good thing I could not talk. That book about sex addiction scared the living crap out of me. I was full of panic, fear, and anxiety as I read about the horrors the author had lived through and what her process of healing was like. I did NOT want to be dealing with what that book described, and it spun me into a state of whole-hearted terror.

Of course, being the mature individual that I was, when I realized my body and mind were going haywire with fear and panic I quit reading, put the book down, and did a few things to calm and ground myself.

No I didn't.

I just kept on reading. That book was a train wreck, and I could not avert my eyes. So, despite the circus of horror happening in my body and brain, I read on, unable to stop, until I was a shaking unglued mess.

I do not recommend this.

While reading books about betrayal trauma, sexual addiction, and infidelity can be a vital part of your healing process, it can also be incredibly triggering, increasing the fear and pain you are experiencing. As such, when reading or listening to material about betrayal trauma, it is incredibly important that you pace yourself. *Taking in more than you can handle in any one sitting is a form of self-harm that is likely to exacerbate the trauma symptoms you are already experiencing.*

If you notice that what you are reading is heightening your feelings of fear, anxiety, panic, and pain, you might want to give yourself a break from the material and do something else for a while, preferably something that might help to calm you down. A few suggestions include yoga, walking, meditation, journaling, calling a friend, taking a bath, deep breathing, and anything else that typically relaxes you.

At this point you might be saying to yourself, "But I *already* feel fear, anxiety, panic, pain, sadness, confusion, etc. What's a little more when I'm dealing with this all the time already?" My response to this is that you are in a chronically heightened fear state, and you need to be careful to not exacerbate things more than necessary. Much of your focus in the early stages of recovery is going to be on trying to calm your body, mind, and emotions down – helping your body and mind manage the hyper-arousal you are experiencing due to the trauma of betrayal. So, reading material that triggers you and increases your hyper-arousal, however enlightening that material might be, can do you more harm than good.

One way to help monitor your level of hyper-arousal is to think about your feelings of fear, anxiety, pain, and panic on a scale of one to ten. As you go through the day, try to pay attention to your thought patterns as you respond to situations, books, audio material, etc. If something causes your level of hyper-arousal and fear to crest past five on your one to ten scale, you need to take a break and do something to calm yourself.

Taking It Easy

Educating yourself, helping you deepen your understanding about who you are, what has happened to you, how your mind and body have been impacted, healthy relationships, repair of relational wounds – these are all essential for your growth and healing. However, the saying, "How do you eat an elephant? One bite at a time," applies not just to pachyderms but also to betrayal trauma. Going slow, taking your time, and allowing yourself the space to absorb and process what you are learning will actually help you move more quickly through the process of healing.

4

TO DO: PROTECT YOUR SEXUAL HEALTH

I t is heartbreaking to realize that your physical safety has been compromised through the sexual behavior of your significant other. No one wants to believe that the person they love, who is supposed to have their back and protect them, has instead put their health and well-being at risk. The shock of this discovery deepens the betrayal and often ignites rage and anger for the partner whose health has been treated so cavalierly.

Sometimes this anger and pain can be paralyzing, blocking your ability to make decisions or take steps to help yourself. Sometimes, the idea that your spouse would engage in sexual behaviors that could cause you serious and life-threating health problems feels too big to even consider. It can feel easier to believe your spouse if he says, "I always used condoms," or, "I never had sex with him/her," because the alternative is too horrifying to accept.

Despite the enormous difficulty of facing this facet of betrayal, it is imperative that you, as the betrayed partner, allow yourself to consider the idea that your health has been put at risk so you can take steps to protect and care for yourself moving forward. Even if your partner claims to have always used condoms or to not have had intercourse, if there has been cheating that involves a live person, it is imperative that you take steps to ensure that your physical health is protected.

Getting Tested

The first step to take is to get tested for Sexually Transmitted Infections. Even if your spouse says he did not put your health at risk, it is vital that you get tested. Your health may or may not have been put at risk. Either way, trusting and depending on the word of your cheating partner is not a wise move at this point. Your health and well-being are of vital importance, and while you did not have a choice about the danger you have been put in, you do have the ability to proactively protect and safeguard yourself now.

Getting tested is not just about your physical safety; it's also about your emotional safety. Getting tested can bring you peace of mind and reassurance by eliminating one more haunting 'what if.' It can also provide you with a sense of empowerment as you act on your own behalf. Even if the results indicate that your health has been compromised, you will be able to advocate for yourself by seeking treatment and getting support.

The next step is to ask your cheating partner to get tested and to request that he allow you to see the doctor's report of the test. You want to ensure that your physical health will not be put on the line if you resume sexual activity with your significant other.

For many betrayed partners, the idea of picking up the phone, making an appointment, and going in to get tested feels daunting. There can be shame around being cheated on. There can be enormous anger over the price you are paying for your cheating partner's behavior. There can be a sense of unfairness that you are experiencing consequences when you have done nothing wrong.

Sometimes these feelings can make it seem too hard to take the steps you need to take, bogging you down in procrastination. One way to help yourself with this is to remind yourself that while you did not get to choose whether you were cheated on, you do get to choose how you respond and move forward. Being cheated on can make you feel worthless and can dent your self-esteem in serious ways. Taking steps to care for yourself, protect yourself, advocate for yourself, and empower yourself affirms that you are indeed worthy, lovable, and precious.

Using Protection

Your next step is to ask your partner to use protection if and when you are sexual together. In the aftermath of betrayal, some couples put sex on hold while they sort out what has happened, determine whether they are staying together or not, and begin to emotionally heal. For these couples, the relationship feels too emotionally unsafe to sustain the vulnerability of being sexual with one another. But other couples continue to be sexual together while sorting out the relational and emotional wounds. For them, sex feels like something that holds the relationship together despite the deep injuries and mistrust that exist.

If you are still being sexual with your cheating partner, your wisest course of action is to insist that barrier protection is used until you have received the results of the STI testing. If your partner has been engaging in sex outside of the relationship compulsively, you will want to use protection throughout early recovery – at least until your addicted partner has established some length of sobriety and you can be assured that his risky behaviors are not continuing. If your partner has been engaged in an affair, you will want to use barrier protection until you are absolutely sure the affair has ended and sex outside of the primary relationship has ceased.

Using condoms is a suggestion that I regularly make to betrayed partners, and I am repeatedly shocked at how few of them have thought of this issue or considered the risk that they are taking by not utilizing protection. I believe this is because it is so painful to contemplate the need for physical protection with their significant other. To need and use condoms is an immediate and terrible reminder of the betrayal that has occurred. As a result, many partners enter into denial around this issue, not letting themselves come into awareness about the risks to their physical health that being sexual with their cheating partner can create.

Betrayed partners have expressed two big hurdles that they run into when they consider setting a boundary with their significant other around the use of condoms or other barrier protection. The first is the fear that they will make their partner angry by insisting that protection be used. For those married to sex addicts, this can be a particularly significant fear, as they have been trained by the addict for many years to put the addict's sexual happiness ahead of their own. As a result, they are afraid that the addicted partner will make them pay in some way for making this request. That he or she will become angry, withdraw relationally, or enact some other some other form of emotional punishment or manipulation.

The second, often even bigger hurdle that betrayed partners experience is the difficulty of coming face to face with a tangible reminder of betrayal in the middle of making love. It is an emotionally jarring experience for betrayed partners when they are in the vulnerability and passion of sex and must suddenly pause for protection to be introduced – protection that is only necessary because of the betrayal and the ongoing lack of safety in the relationship. Continuing to make love can be a challenge when a tangible reminder of danger and pain enters into the experience. Often, this derails arousal and the sense of connection and safety that was present.

You Can Do It

It takes courage to ask for STI testing and to insist that protection be used during sex. It also takes conviction. Conviction that your health and well-being are important and worth protecting. Conviction that you are responsible for taking care of you. Conviction that if your partner cannot participate in protecting your physical health, then he or she is not worthy of being allowed access to you. Conviction that you are precious.

WHAT NOT TO DO: ALLOW BETRAYAL BLINDNESS TO PUT YOU AT RISK

Many betrayed partners enter therapy in a state of shock and disbelief, reeling from the discovery of their partner's extracurricular sexual behaviors. They sit on my couch and tell me they had no idea, not even an inkling, of what their significant other was doing. They have been caught off guard, unaware, and they can't believe this is happening to them.

I listen to their stories, and I know that their shock and bewilderment is real, and they truly did not know what was happening. But, at the same time, I also know that they did know.

I know this because in the weeks that follow they inevitably tell me stories about their relationship and various clues they overlooked. I hear about previous infidelities; about finding pornography, condoms, and secret internet accounts; about changes in the nature of their sex life and their sense of emotional intimacy; about conversations, conflicts, accusations, and denials all indicating the presence of a problem.

Yet they still did not know. Even though they knew.

How does this happen? How do betrayed partners know but not know? And where does the part of them that *does* know go?

In the past, this type of behavior has been labeled "denial" and addressed as a form of codependence on the part of the betrayed partner. Today, thanks to an enormous amount of research, we have new models that help us dig deeper and better understand the function and purpose of these knowing-but-not-knowing behaviors.

Jennifer Freyd, PhD, one of the seminal researchers on the topic of betrayal trauma, has spent years investigating why people don't allow themselves to see the betrayal that is unfolding right in front of their eyes and has coined the term *betrayal blindness* to describe the phenomenon.

Betrayal blindness is not allowing yourself to see what is going on, to connect the dots, or to fully engage with reality, because if you did, the information would threaten your relationship with the person who is most important to you.

What this means is that events or realities that threaten our sense of secure connection to our partner can feel like life or death to us. Whatever the threatening information may be, we can't let ourselves know about it because it would create such chaos, terror, pain, and confusion that we feel we might not survive it emotionally and psychologically.

Instead, we keep the information out, and we don't allow one plus one to ever equal two. By doing this, we keep our world intact. This is a coping mechanism, and it is largely unconscious. We aren't saying to ourselves, "I don't think I'll let myself know about that, thank you very much." Instead, our bodies register that we are in danger, and before the information gets to our conscious minds we instinctually move to protect ourselves by blocking it out, rationalizing it away, or in some way keeping it from landing where we have to fully deal with it.

Betrayal blindness is what makes some partners engage in sexual activity with the cheating partner before getting back the STI results. It is what prevents others from 'remembering' to use condoms during sexual activity. The reality that your physical safety has been put at risk so casually by the person who is supposed to put your well-being above all others is too difficult to know; so, you go blind to it.

The problem with this is that if you are not fully in your reality, you can't make decisions to take care of yourself. When you are blind to what is happening, it puts you and others at emotional, financial, physical, and psychological risk. Situations often get worse when you are in betrayal blindness. The consequences to you and those you love can become even more dire than they already are.

I have sat with too many women who have been diagnosed with cervical cancer from the Human Papillomavirus (HPV) caught through the actions of their cheating partners. The consequences of cheating can be serious and life-threatening, and it is vital that you let yourself know about the risks to your health if you have been betrayed.

Awareness about the phenomena of betrayal blindness and your own ability to enter into betrayal blindness is key during the first stages of recovery. My hope is that even though these issues are painful to look at, you will allow yourself to fully know about potential risks to your physical health. My hope is that you will be brave and take the steps needed to protect yourself. My hope is that you will use your voice and claim your power around your sexual and physical health.

5

TO DO: KNOW WHAT TO EXPECT FROM YOUR CHEATING PARTNER

For betrayed partners who want to try to stay in their relationship and see if healing is possible, there are big questions about what to expect related to their cheating partner's recovery process. The first and most important thing to know is that recovery is not linear. It is more like a hiking trail with a lot of switchbacks, side roads, dead ends, and detours. There are parts of the trail that are difficult and no fun to navigate, but they are nonetheless necessary and a sign of moving forward.

Below, I've tried to give you a sense of what to expect as you and your significant other begin the strange journey called recovery. I have started this discussion with the bad news – the parts that are harder to deal with – to get this out of the way. Then we talk about the good news.

The Bad News: Denial

You can expect to witness a significant amount of denial. For your cheating partner to betray a person he loves (i.e., you), he must lie to and manipulate not just you but himself. He does this by rationalizing, justifying, and minimizing his behaviors. And this long-ingrained stinkin' thinkin' does not change quickly. It is deeply rooted and must repeatedly be confronted and slowly transformed.

I was sitting with a sexually addicted client recently who told me that he had gone back through his email and chat history and was shocked at the number of people he had met with to have sex. He told me that he had been saying to himself that he 'actually cheated' only three or four times. In reality, there were more than two dozen different sex partners in his recent text and chat history. He had hidden from himself what he was doing.

At the beginning of recovery, a cheating partner's denial can take many forms. He can deny that he has a problem, he can deny that he needs help, he can deny that he needs to stop the behaviors, he can deny the level of harm and damage he has done. The very first task in the recovery process is to break through the cheater's denial. If his distorted thinking cannot be arrested, the problematic behaviors will not stop, because denial-based thinking gives him permission to continue those behaviors.

For you as the betrayed partner, it is important to know that in early recovery your cheating partner still has a lot of denial. You will want to make sure you do not collude with this denial by agreeing with any of the distorted thinking that shows up. Furthermore, you should not take on the job of trying to help him see through his denial. Trying to be the person that confronts his denial will only cause you more pain as your trauma symptoms around being lied to and manipulated get reactivated. So, if you can, trust that your partner's therapist, therapy group, 12-step program, and support network are focusing on this task.

The Bad News: Lying

Just like denial, your cheating partner has been lying for a very long time. At the beginning of his recovery, that lying is likely to continue. Even if he has told you the whole truth about the betrayal (which he potentially hasn't), you will continue to catch him lying about many other issues.

This is incredibly emotionally activating for you as the betrayed partner. You already have intolerable pain around the way you have been lied to and had your reality manipulated by your significant other. Continued lying and manipulation just makes it worse. You will probably feel as if the lying must stop immediately or there is no way forward.

Unfortunately, it often takes time for a cheating partner to come to a point of being willing to tell the truth and be fully honest. Most cheating partners, when confronted with questions from a betrayed spouse, respond with dishonesty in an almost habitual pattern. It takes time and intentionality to overcome this automatic impulse to lie and to instead answer questions honestly and forthrightly.

Part of early recovery is learning how to tell the truth regardless of the consequences. The Big Book of AA says that if addicts can be honest they can recover, and if they can't be honest they cannot recover. Learning to be honest and to apply the standard of rigorous honesty to all of life is a big task. It is a skill that must be learned, and that learning takes time. Figuring out how to overcome the immediate impulse to protect oneself by lying is no small feat, and your partner will inevitably make mistakes and missteps along the way. As long as these are used as learning opportunities, there is hope for lasting change.

To you as a betrayed partner, it may feel like knowing and understanding that it takes time to change such a deeply ingrained behavior pattern is the same as giving the cheater permission to continue lying. It isn't. Having clear boundaries and bottom lines that protect you when your partner continues to lie is important. These boundaries help you feel a sense of empowerment and agency in taking care of yourself while your unfaithful partner gets clear with himself and you about the truth.

The Bad News: Bargaining

Along with denial and lying comes bargaining. Bargaining is where your cheating partner tries to find what the Big Book of AA calls an 'easier, softer way' to recover – a way that allows him to get well but to get well his way, without the kind of effort, sacrifice, time, and financial investment that true recovery involves. Bargaining is linked to your partner's desire to continue being the captain of his ship despite the fact that he has rammed it onto the shoals and caused catastrophic loss and damage.

I see this all the time when cheating partners enter treatment at CRR. They give their therapist detailed reasons why they cannot come to therapy every week, why they don't need to be in group therapy, why the 12 steps are not going to work for them, why they don't need to do the homework, etc. In addition to bargaining about treatment, they bargain about their behaviors, saying that the strip clubs and massage parlors are not the real problem and they just need to stop spending so much money on prostitutes, or that the porn and masturbation can continue as long as the in-person extracurricular activities stop.

For your cheating partner, recovery can feel like a new part-time job. He must change his schedule to accommodate therapy and 12-step meetings, create a line item in the budget for treatment, change who he hangs out with as he begins to differentiate between healthy and unhealthy friendships, process tons of new information, and develop a new perspective on life, sex, and relationships. That this amount of intervention is required to create long-term change can be hard to accept. As a result, your partner will very likely bargain with recovery at the beginning, trying to find an easier way.

Bargaining is a normal part of the recovery process. As the betrayed partner, you want to be aware of it and to resist colluding with your cheating partner when he tries to convince you that he doesn't really need the amount of help that is being recommended or tries to talk you into overlooking sexual behaviors that are untenable in your relationship. Having a therapist who can help you set and effectively maintain boundaries can help you resist your cheating partner's efforts to bargain.

. . .

It's Not Easy

Dealing with your cheating partner's denial, lying, and bargaining is difficult. More so because each of these things is part of the betrayal that you have experienced, part of what has caused you deep pain. If you are like I was at the beginning of recovery, you'll just want these things to stop and stop now. Learning that these behaviors take a while to curtail is not welcome news. However, one of the hallmarks of authentic hope is that it is grounded in reality. Rather than wishing for a different situation, authentic hope looks at what the real situation is and deals with it.

As the betrayed partner, what you want to do at the beginning of the recovery process is watch for change rather than perfection. When you look at the big picture, are you seeing improvement in your partner's denial, lying, and bargaining? Are these behaviors showing up less and less? Are you hearing healthier, reality-based talk coming from your partner? Is there more acknowledgment of his problems and the impact his behaviors have had on you and others, including himself? These are the signs to look for. These are the signs that things are moving in the right direction.

The Good News: Willingness

If your partner is taking his need for help seriously and is fully committing to a process of recovery, there are certain things you can expect to see from him. These new behaviors, when you see them, will go a long way toward helping you rebuild a sense of safety.

One of the first things you will see from your recovering partner is willingness. For him, willingness is a major shift in the healing process. For you, willingness indicates he is taking the process of recovery seriously, and he's likely to take the necessary steps toward recovery and healing.

There is a saying in AA that the 'ism' in alcoholism stands for 'I Sponsor Myself.' Before entering recovery, most cheating partners very much embrace the idea that they know what is best for them and they are in charge of themselves, even when they find themselves operating in complete secrecy and isolation in many areas of their lives.

One of the ways you will know your cheating partner is truly committed to repairing the damage he has caused is that he will start to let other people help him steer his ship. He will listen to and hear the advice of wise friends, family, pastors, bosses, etc. He will take in what his therapist says to him, and he will be willing to do the things that are recommended as part of treatment. He will also have the willingness to listen to you, to hear your pain, and to see you as an important ally in the process of recovery.

When willingness comes on board, there is a softening that occurs in your cheating partner. Rather than being hard-edged and defended, he becomes open and interested in advice and direction that might be helpful to him. Rather than trusting only himself (a situation that has not worked so well) he begins to trust others and to try on the suggestions and recommendations they make.

The Good News: Transparency

Another thing you can expect to see with your cheating partner is a new level of transparency. When he was cheating on and betraying you, there were all kinds of opaque and confusing secrets and lies. Because of this, you probably felt like the truth was a phantom you could never pin down. It's likely that you continually had an uneasy feeling that something was wrong, even if you couldn't put a finger on what it was.

Your partner played into this. To keep his infidelity secret, he guarded his phone(s), kept secret bank and credit card accounts, created diversions, and maintained elaborate ruses. Now, if he is committed to recovery and restoration of the relationship, these guarding and defensive behaviors give way to transparency. Technology is left unguarded and open to your perusal. The same is true with financial accounts, your partner's location throughout the day, etc.

There is also a new level of transparency in your conversations.

And this is as helpful for your cheating partner as it is for you. I have had countless cheating partners tell me about the relief they feel when they no longer have to pass every word they say through a filter in their minds, wondering if anything they are saying will give away their secret life.

After discovery and disclosure, your cheating partner can share his thoughts, daily events and happenings, and relationships with you in a much freer and more authentic way. This level of transparency may be experienced viscerally by you. It may feel as if a veil has been lifted or an invisible object that was sitting in the middle of the relationship is no longer there.

The Good News: Accountability

Along with willingness and transparency comes a movement toward accountability. This is a major change from the cowboyed-up attitude of doing whatever is wanted with no thought given to the impact on others. When you see your partner becoming accountable, you know that he is serious about recovery.

Most cheating partners have been accountable to no one, not even themselves. Often, they have violated their own value systems and deeply held beliefs about trust, fidelity, loyalty, and family. They have been caught in the throes of self-will run riot, and they have refused to be subject to the limits and responsibilities that are part of relationships with other people.

In early recovery, a shift from self-will toward accountability takes root. There is a recognition of the deep self-centeredness driving the cheating behaviors, with a commitment to work on and eliminate this character defect. As part of this, there is recognition of the need to be held accountable by others.

Most of us aren't very good at being our own accountability partner. We need the people around us to expect certain things from us, to encourage us toward being our best selves, to remind us of who we want to be when we fail, and to hold our feet to the fire when necessary. Recognition and acceptance of this fact is a significant step forward in your cheating partner's recovery.

As your significant other moves forward in recovery, you will see him let others hold him accountable. You will see him welcome accountability as a beneficial force in his life rather than something to be rebelled against. This shift toward accountability will help him become more congruent – aligning his words, values, and beliefs with his behavior. For you, his willingness to be accountable for his behaviors can provide hope for long-term change and relationship healing.

WHAT NOT TO DO: TRY TO FIND A SHORTCUT

One of the biggest things to expect as you begin to recover from betrayal trauma is that your healing will happen as a process. By definition, processes unfold over time. This means that your individual healing and, potentially, the repair of your relationship are going to happen step by step, moment by moment rather than very quickly as you might hope.

The healing process is not fast and cannot be rushed. It takes time to understand traumatic events and experiences and to integrate them into the narrative of your life. You must grapple with loss. You must wrap your mind around the altered landscape of your life. You must feel your feelings and work through difficult and challenging emotions. You must connect to your longings and imagine a new future, and then you must do the hard work of building that future. This all takes time.

If you are anything like me when I started my recovery process, you will not like the idea that getting out of your painful post-betrayal reality is going to take time. I wanted answers now! I did not have time to deal with a process or walk a path or take a breath. I was in intolerable pain and I needed it to end this freaking minute thank you very much. Anyone who suggested that I needed to slow down and let the process unfold was not welcome at my table. I wanted the fast movers, quick thinkers, and direct talkers to show me the shortcut to making the pain stop and getting my topsy-turvy world right-side-up again. Today.

When I was in this place, I had certain thinking patterns and behaviors that I employed to try to make things go faster and get better quicker. Below are some of the things I thought and tried. See if you recognize any of these in yourself.

Stop It!

My betrayal experience was centered around being married to a sex addict. However, for a long time I did not understand that I was dealing with addiction. And even when I finally let that word in and started to connect the idea of addiction with my situation, I did not really understand what it meant. I had been taught (very erroneously) that to change a behavior you just need to decide to stop doing it. Any understanding of the ways in which behaviors can function unconsciously to benefit us and therefore be deeply entrenched and challenging to change was not something I knew about. And addiction... behavior that is driven by deep unconscious feelings and a neurochemical process in the brain? I had no idea about any of that.

So, for a long time I believed that my husband needed to decide to stop his behaviors. When he did not stop the behaviors, what that meant to me was that he didn't love me enough to stop or that he was an incredibly cruel person who hurt other people willingly. I did not understand that without an immersive series of interventions and treatment he was not going to be able to stop the behaviors. I truly thought that he was in charge of his addiction. I did not understand that his addiction was in charge of him.

Every partner of a sex addict that I've ever worked with has had to go through a similarly steep learning curve about addiction. Most partners who acknowledge that their spouse is dealing with an addiction will tell you that they know what that means. But the reality is that learning about addiction is like taking apart an artichoke. Layer by layer you deepen your knowledge and understanding of what it truly means to be addicted and to recover.

Part of the reason I denied the existence of addiction in my relationship for so long and believed my spouse could just 'stop it' was that I wanted the solution to the problem to be easier than it was. I wanted relief to come sooner and change to happen faster. Which leads us to another thing I tried...

The Fantasy Island Honeymoon

When you are trying to fix the problem as quickly as possible and regain a sense of safety in the relationship, you can sometimes move toward your partner with a great deal of emotional and sexual intensity. Reconnecting with one another closes the relational and emotional gap created by the cheating. It can provide a sense of reassurance that you are still bonded with one another, still love one another, and still want one another despite what has happened.

I have had many betrayed partners tell me that after discovery of the cheating, they and their partner experienced a new level of connection and intimacy that they had not previously known. They talked for hours, their significant other was emotionally plugged in and engaged in a new way. There was romance and hot sex as the couple entered an intensity bubble, seeking to reassure each other that their relationship was still viable.

I like to call this the Fantasy Island honeymoon stage. During this stage, betrayed partners can quickly forgive the cheater in an effort to put the past behind them and move forward together. And why not? Suddenly they have the partner they have always wanted, and the future seems hopeful.

I rarely see couples who are in this stage in my counseling office. Things are going too well. There is a sense that they are working through things and they are going to be able to put all the hurt and pain behind them and move on. The problem has been conquered, they have gotten through it together, so they do not need therapy.

When I do see couples in my office is when this stage ends. And it does inevitably end. The Fantasy Island honeymoon is just not sustainable. In some ways, it is not even real. The changes that occur in the relationship during this stage are crisis and fear driven. The couple is coming together seeking reassurance that the cheating is not going to tear them apart for good. Their acute need for solace, comfort, relief, and reassurance lights a bonfire of intensity that cannot be sustained. Reality eventually creeps into the picture.

There is nothing wrong with this. It is a normal response to finding that your relationship has been pushed to the brink of possible ruin. However, as I said before, it is not sustainable. Eventually, things are going to calm down, the intensity is going to wane, and the fears and doubts that the intensity covered up or distracted you from are going to resurface. This is when a little voice in the back of your head that (for a time) seemed very faint and far away gets closer and louder. Questions like, "How do I know he won't hurt me like that again?" "What actually caused him to cheat?" "How can I trust him again?" and "How can he just stop if he is an addict?" rise to the surface of your mind and present themselves for consideration.

The Fantasy Island honeymoon stage can last different amounts of time for different people. For some couples it lasts a few weeks; for others, it might last for months. But for all couples, the honeymoon eventually ends because the pain of betrayal has not been adequately addressed. Eventually, reality sets in and the betrayed partner realizes that everything is not fixed and much more is needed to move forward in the relationship.

Getting in the Way of Real Help

A couple came for counseling recently looking for help with the husband's sexual addiction. The wife had discovered an extensive history of acting out behavior including porn, cruising, anonymous sex with men, and affairs with women.

They came in, they were assessed, and they began the recovery process. However, as the addicted husband started to settle in and get serious about his addiction and recovery, the wife began telling him that he needed to stop therapy. He was facing the reality of an out-of-control problem and was starting to put in place for himself the interventions and supports recommended by his therapist to help him arrest his behaviors and change his life. But the wife wanted a quicker fix. She, like me at the beginning of my healing journey, did not want a process that took time and included uncertainty. She wanted everything to get better now, even if that meant denying the reality of the addiction. So, she began a campaign to have her husband quit therapy. And guess what? He did.

I don't know what has happened to them. However, I suspect that her desire for the pain and anxiety to end will actually cause even deeper loss and pain in the long run. She and her addicted husband may have to cycle through more rounds of betrayal before she really understands and accepts that his problem is not a quick fix issue and she needs to open herself to the slower but more meaningful process of recovery.

The Secret to Recovery: Slow Down to Go Faster

As you can see from the discussion above, trying to find a short-cut only takes you down multiple dead ends that waste time and energy. This, in my experience, is a paradox of recovery. Going slower and accepting that recovery is a process is the faster route to healing. This is a paradox I've experienced in both my professional and personal life.

Last year, for example, a group of my friends and I decided to work through a book by Tara Mohr called *Playing Big*. This book is for women who want to play bigger in their lives and who, in attempting to do so, run into the inner resistance that nearly always comes when we are stretching ourselves toward something new.

I spent some time with these friends recently, and we talked about the experience of finding our inner mentor, part of chapter two in the book. When I first met my inner mentor in this envisioning exercise, I found that she was a wiser older part of me. She wore very flowy linen clothing and emanated calmness and openness of heart. However, when I looked at her, she looked back at me with worry in her eyes. When I asked her what I need to do to get from where I am today to where I want to be, she told me that I need to slow down. Way down. That I needed to stop striving and struggling so hard to move so many things forward at one time. That I will get where I want to go sooner if I go slower.

As she told me this, I could feel the calmness and peace emanating from her. I could also feel the hurry-up-and-get-it-done-ness emanating from me. However, over time and many years of healing, I have learned to trust my inner voice, so I believed her when she told me that I need to slow down and that I will 'get there' faster if I do.

Of course, understanding that idea is one thing; putting it into practice is a different matter entirely. Because our brains ALWAYS want more. More information, more entertainment, more sex, more food, more things, more distractions, more experiences.

It is a major task to switch from this mode of faster, quicker, bigger, better to a slowed down, embodied, deliberate, and intentional way of living. Yet that is exactly what the most difficult aspects of life require from us – including recovery from betrayal trauma. The healing process asks us to go slowly, to take the time to learn how to be connected to ourselves, possibly for the first time ever. To cut ourselves some slack as we struggle with normal daily life tasks during the first days and weeks after discovery. To be patient with ourselves as we learn new ways of coping. To ease ourselves into relationships with others where we reveal our deep hurts with honesty and vulnerability.

With recovery, going slowly gets us there faster in the end. It gives us space to not just learn new information cognitively but to engage in the experiences that transform us from the inside out. It allows deep and lasting change to occur, instead of quick but temporary alterations that swiftly fade.

Wherever you are in the process of healing, I encourage you to slow down, to pause, and to intentionally tune in to what you need at this particular time and place in your journey. What does your inner voice of wisdom have to say? What is the vision cast by this wiser older part of you? What is revealed when you tap into what you most deeply long for?

As you slow down, remind yourself that you are actually going faster. Because when it comes to recovery, the tortoise always, always wins the race.

6

TO DO: GIVE YOURSELF PERMISSION TO STAY, LEAVE, OR NOT KNOW

One of the biggest issues facing individuals whose relationships have been damaged by a partner's infidelity is the decision to stay in or leave their relationship. The breach of trust created by cheating pushes most relationships to the brink, and betrayed partners must decide if their relationship is fixable and worth saving or if it's broken beyond repair. Below we look at several of the different forces that play a role in making this a complicated question for most partners to answer.

To Stay or To Go: That is the Question

For most betrayed partners it's clear that the future of the relationship has been jeopardized by the loss of trust and safety caused by the lying and cheating. However, they typically do not immediately know what they want to do. Do they want to stay in the relationship? Can they stay in the relationship? Is the relationship too damaged for them to ever trust and feel safe in it? Early on, the answers to these questions are unclear, and as a result there is uncertainty and anxiety about how to move forward.

Complicating this uncertainty is the added layer of shame with which betrayed partners often struggle. They are affected by the sometimes very strongly held cultural belief that if you are cheated on, you must leave the cheater, and if you don't, you are weak.

I'll give you an example. I was talking with one of my clients about how angry and shaming she was being to her sexually addicted spouse. The couple had been working on their recovery for over a year. He had established sobriety, and the relationship was improving. However, she would occasionally give him a thorough down-and-dirty tongue lashing that would leave both of them emotionally reeling for days.

I asked her what she thought this behavior was about. She told me, "You know what it is? I don't just feel like I have a right to hurt him because of his cheating; I feel like I have an obligation to hurt him. I feel like I'm supposed to make him pay. If I don't, I am a weak and a stupid fool for staying with him, and I am just letting him walk all over me in the relationship."

On television and in movies, you often see the "leaving after infidelity" storyline portrayed. A partner is unfaithful. The victim of this betrayal is a self-respecting woman who gathers up her cloak of pride and stalks out of the relationship, looking for greener pastures elsewhere. Only rarely do you see depictions of couples affected by cheating who stay together and work through the pain.

If the media portrayals aren't enough, friends and family often jump to the same conclusion. With little to no understanding of your situation, they advise you to leave your relationship. They almost never suggest that you might want to stick it out, grow from the experience, and develop a relationship that is stronger and more meaningful because you've overcome adversity in it.

Despite the cultural story and advice that is so prevalent, most people try hard to find a way to stay in their relationship. Our attachment to our significant other is the organizing relationship in our life and the place where our deepest emotional needs are expressed. It provides us with a sense of security and safety, acting as the safe base from which we launch ourselves into the rest of our lives. Severing this attachment completely (through breakup or divorce) is not something that most of us do lightly or easily.

Until you have been in the situation yourself and faced the details of a shared reality (children, a mortgage, good memories, love and affection for your partner, a close relationship with your in-laws, financial obligations, etc.), you can't possibly know what you would, could, or should do. The simple truth is that most people, no matter how badly they've been betrayed, want their relationship to work. Most are looking for a way to stay together, even in the face of relational trauma.

That said, after discovering betrayal, leaving can initially feel like the right thing to do. It can seem like a viable way to save your pride and take yourself out of pain and confusion. And for some betrayed partners, leaving is indeed the best course of action. But for many other betrayed partners, making such a huge, life-altering decision while smack in the middle of a major crisis is not the wisest choice.

Whatever you choose, it is your decision. And it is not weak to choose to stay in your relationship. I am amazed every day by the strength and grace of the women I sit with who, despite being dealt a cruel hand, choose to stay in their relationship. They knowingly take on the difficult task of opening themselves up to new ways of thinking and stretching toward growth and change so they can (hopefully) heal. This takes bravery, patience, fortitude, and a willingness to become vulnerable despite daunting odds. It requires a belief that hope for healing, repair, forgiveness, and reconciliation is the birthplace of true possibility. It is not an act of weakness to stay, and there is no shame in it.

In the same way, it is not weak to choose to leave. Sometimes, the greatest act of self-care is the courageous choice to end a destructive relationship and lean into the task of rebuilding a new and different life. Leaving someone you love, grieving the loss of the relationship and its attendant hopes and dreams, and then embracing the process of building a new life as a single person initially and then re-engaging in a new and hopefully healthier relationship: These are not small tasks. So, the choice to leave, much like the choice to stay, requires courage, patience, wisdom, and strength.

If you feel like the choice that you have made is a sign of weakness and that you are letting your dignity be trampled on, I encourage you to reframe how you are thinking about this issue. No one can make this choice for you. Only you truly understand all that is at stake in the decision to leave or to stay. Only you know the depth of courage it takes to make your decision. Hopefully, you have wise friends and supportive counsel around you as you make and process your decision – people who understand that ultimately you are the one who will live with this choice, people who understand that both choices are valid. There is no shame in staying, and there is no shame in leaving.

Stay or Leave: Permission to Not Know

In the immediate aftermath of discovering betrayal, emotions run high for both the betrayed partner and the offending partner. There is chaos and confusion about what has happened and what to do about it.

For many betrayed partners, there can be a sense of pressure to know what they are going to do. However, the reality is that most betrayed partners don't know and, for a time, won't know what the best decision is for them and their relationship. It takes time to wrap your mind and heart around what has happened in the relationship. It takes time to process the level of hurt, pain, and loss created by the betrayal, and to assimilate and integrate this new reality into your current understanding of your life and relationship.

It also takes time to find out the full truth about the scope and depth of the betrayal. It takes time to discover how your cheating partner is going to deal with the betrayal. It takes time to see if your cheating partner wants and is willing to work on repairing your relationship in ways that make staying together possible.

If you're like most betrayed partners, these different facets of dealing with and healing after betrayal create a period of time where you simply do not know whether you want to and can stay in the relationship or need to leave it.

That said, you would probably like certainty. Certainty gives you a sense of knowledge and purpose in the direction you are heading. Uncertainty, on the other hand, often creates insecurity, fear, and anxiety. So, the period of uncertainty about the future of your relationship that you are likely to have can create fear and anxiety. When those feelings are added to the cultural pressure to leave the relationship, you may feel pressured to come up with an answer now. You might also feel like something is wrong with you because you're not ready to decide.

Please hear me: Nothing is wrong with you. Not knowing whether to stay or leave your relationship is completely normal. Most betrayed partners experience a prolonged period of not knowing. You are allowed to take as much time as you need to determine whether your relationship can once again be safe enough for you to stay, or whether relational safety has been damaged beyond repair.

Making the right choice for you and your relationship takes time. There is no way to know at the moment of discovery what needs to happen, or even what you want to happen. The situation must unfold, and, in this unfolding, it will eventually become clear to you how to move forward.

Am I Staying Forever?

As noted above, after discovery of infidelity, betrayed partners often feel pressured to make a black and white decision about leaving or staying in their relationship. Adding to this pressure is a sense that if they decide to stay, they are deciding to stay for all time. And the same is true with leaving. There is a sense that if they leave, they must leave for forever.

As for leaving, it is true that divorce is a rather permanent decision. However, there are lots of ways to create relational space temporarily while you sort out the longer-term decisions. While you make up your mind about trying to make it work versus divorcing, you can try an in-house separation, a therapeutic separation, living in separate residences for a while, and various other options.

A decision to stay is equally a for-the-moment decision. For those who decide to stay in their relationship, the decision can be (and usually is) a decision for the present, not a decision for the future.

I remember one of my clients who was grappling with this issue. She was more than two years past discovery of the betrayal. She had stayed through disclosure of her spouse's sexual addiction and all the incredibly difficult and painful initial actions of recovery. She had clearly decided to stay in her relationship. Yet there we were, two years in, with her telling me how tormented she felt about whether to stay in or leave her relationship. Her behavior to that point clearly said she was staying, but her heart continued to wrestle with the issue.

As we began to name and discuss the emotions wrapped up in this decision, I saw that she was wrestling with the idea of permanence in her relationship. She had an unconscious belief that if she stayed for now, she was deciding to stay forever.

The reality is that none of us knows what is around life's next corner. Disasters happen, deaths occur, betrayal devastates. When we decide to stay in our relationship, we are deciding for the present with an intention toward our future. But none of us can know what the future actually holds. It could be that our straying spouse strays again and at that point we choose to leave. It could be that one of us gets sick and dies and the relationship ends for that reason. It could be that we stay together and die in bed, side-by-side, at the ripe old age of 90 like that couple in the movie *The Notebook*. We don't know. We can't know. We are all living in uncertainty.

So, if you are struggling with the pressure to know, and the decision to stay or go feels final and permanent, allow me to reframe your thinking. Instead of making a permanent decision, what if you decide to stay for now, with the intention of building a healthy, trusting, long-term relationship together.

This option is not a way to take your marriage vows less seriously, by the way. It is actually a way of taking your vows more seriously, living them each day with the intention of building a bridge, day-by-day, to a 20-year or 35-year or 50-year relationship. But your focus is on the present, not the future. Your focus is on what is best for you and your relationship today. You are living in the present with the knowledge and understanding that you don't know what the future holds.

This brings us to another issue that many partners wrestle with around the decision to stay or leave: Should I cut my losses?

Should I Cut My Losses?

"Should I cut my losses and leave now?" If you've asked this question, you're not alone. Many if not most betrayed partners wrestle with thoughts about whether they should cut their losses and leave their relationship now or stay and potentially need to leave later if things break bad down the road.

At heart, this question is about the uncertainty that is unfolding in your relationship. After betrayal, everything feels uncertain. Will your cheating partner want to save the relationship? Do you want to save the relationship? Will the two of you, working together, be able to heal the damage of infidelity and repair your intimate bond? These questions often take time to answer, and even after they're answered the ultimate outcomes are not always clear.

Because of this, there is typically a period of waiting after betrayal. The 'wait and see' time when you are exploring your options and evaluating your partner's intentions. Even if both of you have declared your commitment to work on the relationship and stay together, there is a period when it is not clear if you will be able to do this successfully. Emotions run high, the pain is immense, and the work is hard. What if it doesn't work out?

So betrayed partners often ask, "Should I cut my losses and leave?" But what they are really asking is, "Can I tolerate this uncertainty? Can I roll the dice and bet again on someone who has just hurt me? Can I bear it if we try and then don't make it?"

Think of the words that betrayed partners are actually saying.

Cut. My. Losses. They are literally asking if they should cut out the potential for further loss. Should they accept the loss they have already incurred and limit their potential for further hurt and pain by counting the cost and leaving now?

When you ask this question, you are evaluating your capacity for disappointment. What will happen to you if you allow yourself to hope, to take another risk, and then you are once again devastated with disappointment and loss? Can you bear it?

One of the hardest things about this question is that there is no answer that does not involve the possibility of loss. No matter how you answer the question, you are taking a risk. If you leave, you risk losing a relationship that might have been savable and eventually even great. If you stay, you risk disappointment and loss of hope if you must leave down the road.

What a hard choice. No wonder betrayed partners wrestle so deeply with the question of whether to stay or leave.

Your energy and capacity for hope, disappointment, and risk-taking is unique to you and your circumstance. You are you, and you must make your decision based on who you are and what your life looks and feels like. You can leave or stay, whatever is best for you, and no one can make this choice for you.

As an example, I will offer you my own story. Years ago, when I was married to a sex addict, I stayed and tried, and I tried and stayed. For a long time. Until it was clear that I had to leave.

It would be easy to look back on that 'trying and staying' time as a wasted period in my life. However, that was so incredibly not my experience. During that time, I learned enormous amounts about myself and who I am. I learned about healthy relationships. I learned how to value myself based on my inherent worth rather than how I was being treated. I learned how to be kind to myself and to nurture and care for myself. I broke free from shame. I claimed my voice and my power as a woman. I learned how to give myself permission to fail and be imperfect. I grew. A lot.

In the process of healing from betrayal trauma, regardless of whether you leave now or stay and try to make things work, there is no such thing as wasted time. Everything that is happening, however your personal journey unfolds, will be used in your life to help you grow into more of your true authentic self – if you will allow it. So, if you stay, and then you eventually must leave, you will not have wasted your time. All that you learn and the ways that you change will become part of your story and will shape who you are going forward. Nothing will be lost, and nothing will be wasted. Do not fear that you will waste your time, because on the path of healing there is no such thing.

WHAT NOT TO DO: MAKE BIG DECISIONS FAST

Humans do not like uncertainty. We like a clear direction. An arrow pointing the way. A road that is paved and marked with bright yellow stripes showing us where to go. As a result, when we experience uncertainty we often make hasty decisions, simply to try to eliminate the anxiety that uncertainty creates. Never mind if it is a good decision. At least we chose a fork in the road and are heading somewhere instead of dithering around with our fear while trying to figure out what to do.

The instinct and impulse to find a way out of anxiety and uncertainty is what causes some betrayed partners to make fast decisions about their relationship in the aftermath of betrayal. Choosing to leave or declaring that you are staying can feel like at least it points your feet in a direction.

I was talking with one of my clients about the issue of uncertainty, and she told me, "At the beginning, right after discovery of my husband's affairs, I didn't care if I was doing the wrong thing. I just felt like I had to do *something*. Not doing anything felt powerless and helpless and I couldn't stand it. I had to take action, even if I was going to regret it later."

Discovering betrayal is a little like being thrown out of a boat into a stormy ocean. You have no safety, your life is at risk, and even though you may not know what to do it is imperative that you do something, or you will surely drown.

To be told in the middle of being tossed about by the wind and waves that you should try being still, taking a breath, and getting your bearings can feel insane. But it could also save your life.

Learning about your partner's infidelity is the same. In the middle of so much change, loss, fear, doubt, and uncertainty, it is vital that you take a beat, a moment to stop flailing about trying to figure out what to do at the big picture level of your life (to stay or leave the relationship). You need to focus on your present moment – what do you need to do *right now* to help yourself. You must ask, "What will bring me just a smidge of comfort, clarity, calm, and relief?"

In 12-step fellowships there is a saying that goes, "Do the next right thing." Applying this saying to my own circumstances, whatever my circumstances have been, has helped me many times to step out of the crazy-making anxiety of trying to figure things out, to come into my present moment, and to start living in connected awareness to what I need right now.

Sometimes I find I need a drink, or a nap, or a snack, or a hug, or a conversation with someone close to me. Sometimes I need to take a walk or play for a while to let off some steam. Sometimes I need sleep, or to journal my thoughts, or to cry, or to throw rocks in a pond while being angry. Sometimes I need to laugh, to be entertained. Sometimes I need the peace and quiet of a gentle night on my porch.

The point is that when we come into our present moment and focus on what we need right now, it brings us out of our anxious minds. Our minds often worry about decisions that we do not yet have the information to make. This type of worry, before we are actually equipped to take action, creates suffering.

Doing the next right thing brings us out of our busy-mind, down into our bodies where we can connect with ourselves and care for ourselves with loving kindness. This helps us get our bearings, calm ourselves, and fill our empty tanks.

Only when we are being responsive to our immediate, in the moment needs do we have the resources and energy to take stock of where we are and fully consider the larger questions that are in front of us.

A second issue to consider is that big decisions often require time. Big decisions such as staying or leaving your relationship are life-changing. They are significant. They need reflection and time and space to be fully considered.

Often when we are making big decisions, whether about our relationship, or moving somewhere, or changing jobs, or having a child, etc., we need to try those decisions on mentally and emotionally for a while before we know if they are right for us. To do this, we need space and time for mental and emotional reflection. We need to be able to walk around the issue, consider it from all sides, imagine ourselves in the changed circumstances that the decision will create, and feel our hearts whisper wisdom to us about what we are to do.

This cannot happen in a rush. It cannot happen when driven by fear and anxiety. We can only give ourselves the ability to thoroughly consider big decisions by giving ourselves plenty of time and space. No deadline. No agenda. No swirling, racing, busy-mind cornucopia of anxiety.

So, if you are dealing with betrayal and facing one of the biggest questions that arises from being cheated on (do I stay or leave?), please be gentle with yourself. Acknowledge that this is a big question and that it comes with fear and anxiety and uncertainty. Allow yourself to feel the fear and uncertainty and hold those feelings with kindness and understanding if you can. Then give yourself permission to take care of what you need right now to stabilize emotionally and fully consider the question in front of you. Then give yourself even more permission to wait until you know your decision is the right one before making it, taking all the space and time you need to determine what is best for you. Give yourself the room to be in a process that unfolds over time and know that opting to 'wait and see' is not doing nothing. Instead, it is an active, intentional, grounded-in-awareness choice, and you will be glad you made it.

7

TO DO: KNOW WHAT YOU HAVE A RIGHT TO KNOW

L et's talk about what you, as a betrayed partner, have a right to know about and be involved in when it comes to your unfaithful partner's healing process.

This topic can be very confusing for a lot of betrayed partners. For instance, you may have a spouse who is participating in a 12-Step program who keeps telling you, "You are not supposed to be in my program. You need to stay on your side of the street." Or you may be participating in your own recovery program and hearing something similar from your support network there.

This can make you feel like you do not have the right to know about or provide feedback regarding your significant other's path of recovery. And this can feel very unfair and restrictive.

While it is true that you cannot be in charge of your spouse's recovery, telling him what to do and when to do it, you do, as the betrayed partner, have a right (and I would argue a need) to be informed and involved in his recovery process.

The reality is that if you are trying to stay in your relationship, you're in a Venn diagram of recovery and healing that involves your individual recovery, your significant other's individual recovery, and your recovery together as a couple. These three facets of healing should not be thought of as separate entities but as overlapping circles that form a holistic healing process.

Your individual recovery greatly impacts your relationship and needs to be incorporated into the work that you and your partner do as a couple. The same is true with your significant other's recovery. Moreover, your recovery impacts his recovery, and his recovery impacts yours. And because of this, you have a right to know what is happening in his process of healing, and he has a right to what's happening with you. You each need ways to weigh in and provide information and feedback about decisions that are being made and whatever else is unfolding.

Below are a few of the things that you have a right to ask about and to have honest, forthright conversations with your cheating partner about.

Therapy

You have a right to know who your partner is seeing for therapy, what their credentials are, and how they approach the issue of treating infidelity and betrayal. You have a right to ask to meet this individual so you can increase your comfort level and trust. You have a right to ask your partner what he is working on in therapy and to expect him to share with you about what he is learning. A word to the wise, though: Pick a sensitive and appropriate time to ask your partner about therapy if you choose to do so. Most people need some time to process and absorb the content and emotions resulting from a therapy session. So a phone call to your partner right after his session or a series of pointed questions that evening are probably not going to get you the best information. Give him time to process what was talked about and to come to a place where he is ready and able to share it with you.

12-Step Meetings

If your partner is participating in a 12-Step program, you have a right to know which meetings he is attending. You also have a right to know if he has a sponsor, what that sponsor's first name is, a little bit about who that sponsor is (is he a married lawyer in his 50s, a 28-year-old single firefighter, or a 44-year-old mother of three), and what qualifies that individual to be a sponsor (does he have other sponsees, does he have his own sponsor, how long has he been in the program, does he have a good amount of sobriety). Over time, the sponsor might become important not just to your partner but to you. Frequently, you will begin to see your partner's sponsor as a valuable resource in helping your partner deal with his most troubling issues and behaviors.

Your Physical Safety

We talked about this earlier, but it is worth mentioning again here. If your partner has had sex with someone outside of your relationship, you have a right to ask him to get tested for Sexually Transmitted Infections and to share the results of the test with you. Even if your partner is claiming to have only had protected sex, it is recommended that you request STI testing and to see the results. Your physical safety is a top priority, and you have a right to know if your partner's behavior has put your health at risk.

Sexual Sobriety

If your partner is a sex addict, you have a right to know what his definition of sexual sobriety is. You also have a right to provide feedback about his definition of sexual sobriety. If your partner comes to you and says, "I've defined sexual sobriety as no sex outside of our relationship," but you know that historically he has spent significant amounts of time compulsively masturbating and looking at porn, you might not feel good about his definition. If so, you have the right to say, "I would feel safer and more secure in our relationship if you would specifically include porn and masturbation in your sexual sobriety definition." Your spouse will then have to decide if he wants to amend his sobriety definition. Hopefully, the two of you will be able to engage in a discussion about what sexual sobriety means to each of you, what you want your sexual relationship to look like, and what is needed for emotional safety to be restored.

If your significant other has engaged in infidelity but is not a sex addict, you have a right to discuss, negotiate and fully understand your partner's understanding of your relationship agreements, how cheating and infidelity are defined, and what degree of fidelity you can expect from your partner going forward.

You also have the right to know if your partner has lost his sobriety or cheated again. That said, you must think carefully about what you need to know about this. To this end, you should consider the behaviors that might impact your ability to feel emotionally and physically safe in the relationship. For example, if your addicted spouse has a slip that involves viewing pornography or masturbating (if those are behaviors he has agreed to avoid), you might feel that you do not need to know about this as long as he is being honest with his therapist, sponsor, and recovery community, and working it through. If, however, his loss of sobriety involves hooking up with a former affair partner, this is something you would probably have strong feelings about and would want to know about so that you could make fully-informed decisions about your relationship.

Sexual Behaviors

You have a right to know about the scope and breadth of your spouse's acting out behaviors. We are going to unpack this idea much more thoroughly in the next chapter, so for now let me just affirm your right to know and understand exactly how the relationship agreements have been broken and the extent to which your significant other has lied to and manipulated you.

WHAT NOT TO DO: IGNORE YOUR GUT

For many betrayed partners, the adage about hindsight being 20/20 feels very true. They look back after discovering infidelity and see so clearly all the little signs and indications pointing toward their significant other's betrayal. They remember their feelings of unease, discomfort, fear, anxiety, uncertainty, doubt, and confusion. Then they remember how they chose to ignore what their gut was telling them because they didn't want it to be true.

Consider the following stories:

- Joe lost his job because he was viewing pornography at work. His wife, Sandy, believed him when he said he was just looking at an email someone sent him, it was only that one time, and how crazy and unjust was it that his company fired him? Sandy joined Joe in telling everyone that he was fired unfairly, and they were thinking about suing the company. In reality, Joe was viewing porn at work 7-8 hours a day on average. He knew that he was fired with reasonable cause but he did not want Sandy to find out about his problem, so he lied. Meanwhile, Sandy's gut was telling her there was no way a company could get away with firing someone for one email, but she pushed this down because it was too scary to think about what might really have happened.
- Jennifer noticed that her spouse Keith used sexual jokes and innuendo often in conversation with their friends. He also flirted shamelessly with friends, coworkers, waitresses, etc. Jennifer noticed that some of their friends reacted negatively to Keith's sexual comments. She felt embarrassed and wondered if maybe there was something more going on. When she asked Keith about it, he told her she was being too sensitive, and he was just fooling around and having some fun. Jennifer chastised herself for being paranoid and decided their friends' discomfort

meant something was wrong with them. She decided she was going to try to loosen up and not be such a downer.

- Sharon's husband Bob asked her to view pornography with him to enhance their sex life. She wanted to make him happy, so she agreed. They viewed the porn and had sex, but she did not enjoy it, feeling a nagging sense of discomfort and sadness. Bob, however, was thrilled with the experiment, and a few days later he initiated sex again with the use of porn. Within a few weeks, they were having sex only with porn. Sharon began to feel like little more than a receptacle. When she mentioned this to Bob, he told her, "Everyone uses porn, many people recommend it for the enhancement of sex, and if you were more secure with yourself you would be okay with it." Sharon continued to have sex with Bob while viewing the pornography and tried to talk herself into feeling okay about it. To help herself loosen up, she started drinking several glasses of wine before sex.

Sandy, Jennifer, and Sharon all ignored their inner sense of discomfort, their inner knowledge that something was wrong in their relationship. In other words, they ignored their gut, the inner voice of knowing that speaks up and tries to make itself heard to help you stay in awareness about your reality so you can make good decisions for yourself as life unfolds.

As the well-known author M. Scott Peck once wrote, "Mental health is a commitment to reality at all times." The role of your gut is to help you stay planted in your reality, to notice what is happening, and to connect you to your inner wisdom about how to proceed. Sadly, many of us have never learned how to tune in and listen to this inner voice of truth. Even more tragic, many of us have been taught to actively dismiss or doubt our gut reactions, to trust what others are telling us more, and to prioritize someone else's reality over our own.

In the examples above, you can clearly see the ways in which this occurred. Sandy's gut told her that Joe was lying about why he was fired and there was a bigger, secret problem. Jennifer's gut signaled her discomfort with Keith's sexualizing of people and situations and that his behavior was a sign of a deeper issue. Sharon's gut told her that using pornography as part of her sex life was not good for her and did not enhance or increase her sexual satisfaction and sense of intimacy with Bob, and that his ardent desire to use it might indicate deeper issues. Nevertheless, each of these women doubted her gut, repressed her gut, and even turned on her gut by shaming or otherwise chastising herself for the doubts and uncertainties she was having.

Sadly, this is not uncommon. In fact, most betrayed partners have similar stories. They talk about the ways they talked themselves out of or allowed their cheating partner to talk them out of what they knew in their gut to be true.

It would be lovely as betrayed partners to get a do-over, to go back in time and listen to the inner voice of wisdom, believing it, trusting it, and taking whatever action would have been appropriate. But that is not possible. What we can do is take an honest look back at what happened, allowing ourselves to learn and grow from what we experienced. This means looking at the ways in which we ignored or silenced our gut and asking hard questions of ourselves, such as:

- What did I tell myself to talk myself out of my reality?
- Why was I afraid to trust my gut?
- What was I afraid of?
- Why did I believe my partner more than myself?
- What would I have lost if I had believed myself?
- What would I have had to face or feel if I had trusted my inner voice?

Asking these questions of yourself is so important in early recovery. The process of being curious about how the cheating has unfolded unbeknownst to you and when and how you may have ignored the prompting of that inner nudge that is your gut is vital to coming fully into your reality.

I put the 'to do' of knowing what you have a right to know together with the 'what not to do' of ignoring your gut because it can be scary to lean into knowing. Sometimes it feels safer to not know what your partner is working on or how he has defined sobriety or what he considers cheating. These can be difficult, anxiety-producing conversions. Your gut may be signaling to you that there is an important conversation that needs to occur or a significant question that you need to ask, and you may find yourself trying to quash your gut because it feels too scary.

I understand this only too well. It *is* scary. There is a lot on the line. But it is important to remember that not knowing is even scarier. Not knowing means you cannot take steps to take care of yourself. Not knowing means you cannot set an appropriate boundary, ask for change, make new arrangements, act on your own behalf. Not knowing can feel safer, but it isn't. Knowing what you have a right to know and trusting your gut when it signals that something needs your attention are vital tools for surviving betrayal and moving forward toward healing.

8

TO DO: ASK FOR THE WHOLE TRUTH

After learning about infidelity, most betrayed partners feel an intense need to know the scope and depth of what has happened. The discovery of being lied to, sometimes for years or even decades, and the resulting sense of reality fragmentation leaves them shocked, destabilized, and overwhelmed. It often feels like finding out the whole truth about what has happened, getting every single detail in place, is the only way to escape the insanity and return to a place where reality once more seems knowable. At times, piecing together the truth feels like the only way to piece yourself back together again.

As a betrayed partner, this is not just a need that you have, it is your right within your relationship. You have a right to know if your significant other has broken your relationship agreements, lied to you, and betrayed your trust. You have a right to know how long that has been going on, how the agreements have been broken, and with whom.

When your partner secretly breaks the relationship vows or agreements that are the basis of trust and safety in your relationship, it puts him in a 'one-up' position. He is the only one who knows the whole truth about the relationship and his betrayal. As a result, the relationship is no longer an emotionally level playing field.

To level the playing field, you have a right to know what has happened and how your relationship agreements have been broken. You have a right to know what the full reality of your relationship is, including the full extent of your partner's betrayal, so you can make informed decisions about whether you want to continue in the relationship, how you want to continue in the relationship, and what you need to take care of yourself moving forward.

Now, if only things were this simple.

Where your right to information as a betrayed partner becomes a sticky, tricky issue is when it runs into the brick wall of your significant other's ongoing sexual addiction/cheating and/or his intense fear of losing the relationship. These two things, combo-plattered together, often mean your partner is still keeping secrets and telling half-truths in an effort to convince you that the half-story you are getting is actually the whole whopping tale.

While you are desperately trying to figure out what has happened and to determine what it means for you, your unfaithful mate may be unable to see through the fog of his addiction/infidelity and his fear of losing you. Thus, he may be unable to provide you with the whole honest truth.

I have seen articles posted on the internet and in books written for betrayed partners where the author is adamantly advocating for the betrayed partner to know the full truth of what has happened in the relationship. These writers talk about the right of the betrayed partner to know and the duty of therapists to facilitate the process of full disclosure. I agree with them. However, what is often left out of these discussions is this dicey issue of two people, the betrayer and the betrayed, who are usually in very different places after initial discovery. So, I ask: What happens when your right to know collides with the cheater's reluctance to disclose the entire truth?

The Betrayer's Dilemma

Several years ago, I worked with a client (let's call her Marissa) who discovered through some world-class sleuthing that her spouse (let's call him Mark) had been having anonymous sex with strangers that he met online or picked up in bars. Once Mark knew the jig was up, he confessed to having anonymous sex since the beginning of their dating-engagement-married life together, but he was sketchy with details. During the hours of discussion that followed, Marissa desperately tried to learn the complete truth about Mark's infidelity. The conversation alternated between bouts of angry yelling and painful tears cried together.

The next morning, Marissa called and made therapy appointments for herself and Mark, and they entered treatment. Marissa came to her appointment stuck in a nightmare of fear and pain, feeling like she knew part of the story from what Mark had confessed, but not everything. She felt like there was more. She was also having a hard time holding on to and making sense of what she did know because she was in shock and emotional overwhelm. Still, she knew she wanted the full truth. She had many questions about when, where, who, how many, how often, etc. And it felt absolutely imperative to her that she get honest and complete answers to these questions as soon as possible so she could ground herself in the facts and stop the swirling chaos of being lied to.

Mark, on the other hand, came into treatment knowing he had been caught and that his relationship was on the line. He knew that he had to do something or he was going to lose Marissa and his family, and that terrified him. He felt terrible about the pain he had caused Marissa, and he was shocked at the level of hurt and damage she felt. He wanted to stop the pain and somehow put the genie back into the bottle. He did not, however, want to disclose any more about his infidelity than what he absolutely had to, nor did he want to stop cheating.

Mark was facing the classic cheater's dilemma, which goes like this: "I don't want to hurt my partner, and I'm terribly upset that she is in pain and our relationship is in jeopardy. I also don't want to lose my relationship. However, I cannot give up my sexual behaviors because that is the way I cope with and handle the stress and anxiety of my life."

Typically, the cheater's dilemma occurs because the cheater is attached to two things: his partner and his extracurricular sexual behaviors. These two things are now in conflict, and he is being presented with a choice: his sexual behavior or his relationship.

At this stage of crisis, almost all cheating partners (especially if there is an element of sexual compulsivity) will try to find a way to keep both their relationship and their sexual behavior. And even if they are giving up the infidelity, they at least want to keep some secrets about what they did.

To do this, they make heroic efforts to try to calm their partner and ease her fears while simultaneously protecting and hiding their sexual behaviors and/or secrets. Usually, this involves telling some portion of the truth while maintaining a stash of lies about the full extent and scope of their behaviors. And this partial truth is almost always presented as the full truth, with the cheating partner swearing on the family Bible and crying crocodile tears of remorse to convince the betrayed partner that she now knows everything there is to know.

Can you begin to see the sticky, tricky issue that couples dealing with betrayal can get stuck in? Marissa wanted and needed to know what was happening in her relationship. She also had a right to know this information. She'd been blindsided and tumbled about and for her, it felt like the only way to return to solid ground was to know the entire truth about the betrayal. Meanwhile, Mark was terrified that he might lose Marissa or have to give up his sexual behaviors. It felt to him like telling the truth was the surest way to lose one or the other or both, and his safest course of action was to continue keeping secrets, disclosing only what he absolutely had to tell. He thought that if Marissa knew the full truth, she would stop loving him, lose respect for him, and leave him.

You Can't Make Somebody Tell the Truth

In this dynamic, your cheating partner is often working hard to minimize the damage caused by the discovery of his behavior. Mistakenly, he believes that the way to minimize damage and prevent the loss of his relationship is to continue lying and withholding information. Usually, he does this because he is terrified of losing the relationship. He sees the amount of pain and damage he has caused you, and he has great fear about increasing your level of anguish by revealing more information. As a result, he keeps secrets and continues to lie, hoping the whole story will never be discovered.

Moreover, because of the months, years, or decades spent lying to and manipulating not only you but himself, the instinct to lie, hide, distract, rationalize, minimize, and justify is so strong that he may be doing it unconsciously in a kneejerk, habitual fashion. His long-standing pattern of deception has convinced him that telling the truth is the most dangerous and damaging thing he could possibly do and that lying and hiding is the safest path.

This is the exact opposite of what is actually true. Over and over at CRR, my team and I work with sex addicts and other unfaithful individuals who are convinced that telling the truth will end their relationship. We spend a great deal of time helping them see that it is not what they did that will end the relationship, it's their continued dishonesty. Telling the truth is not what ends relationships; it's continuing to lie and keep secrets that makes a relationship unsustainable for betrayed partners. Almost every relationship that I have watched end has terminated not because of the sexual behaviors, and not because the cheater told the truth about those behaviors, but because of ongoing secrets, manipulation, and deception.

Betrayed partners cannot find any kind of safe emotional ground within the relationship if they are still being lied to, so eventually they give up and end the relationship.

Thus, we are back to our sticky, tricky issue: Betrayed partners want and need full disclosure about the betrayal, but cheating partners are afraid and unwilling to tell the whole truth. And here is the cold, hard, very unwelcome fact that betrayed partners must face: You cannot make your significant other tell you the truth.

Despite your right as a betrayed partner to know the full truth about what has happened in your relationship, despite your emotional and psychological need to receive full disclosure about the betrayal, despite the reality that honesty, truthfulness, and restored integrity are the only possible way forward in the relationship, you cannot make your cheating partner tell you the truth if he is unwilling to do so. And this leads us straight into our 'what not to do' recommendation: Do not expose yourself to further trauma.

WHAT NOT TO DO: EXPOSE YOURSELF TO FURTHER TRAUMA

If you have a right to know but your cheating partner is not yet willing to tell the whole truth about the betrayal, what are you to do?

This dilemma leaves many betrayed partners in a terrible bind. Do you accept the half-truths your significant other is willing to disclose and try to convince yourself that this is the whole truth even when your instincts scream this is not the case? Do you demand, nag, beg, argue, and try to force your significant other tell you the entire truth? Do you borrow a page from Sherlock Holmes and become a master sleuth, trying to figure out reality on your own? Do you exit the relationship, never knowing the whole truth but extricating yourself from the pain of continued confusion and chaos?

Most betrayed partners stuck in this dilemma have tried all of the above and more. Often, as a result, they experience what we refer to in the sexual addiction and infidelity treatment field as staggered discovery. I like to call this death by papercut, as it is a torturous and damaging process.

Staggered discovery looks like this.

You, the betrayed partner, are filled with your need and right to know what has happened. So, you go after it. You are creative, smart, and most of all motivated, and you begin a campaign to wring the truth out of your significant other – by hook, crook, or trick.

You interrogate him like a special agent on speed. You rage, you explain, you argue. You are sweet and try to catch him off guard, seeing if he trips up and tells you something new. You set up cameras, you pretend to be someone else and chat him up online, you put keyboard trackers on his devices, you put a tracker on his car, you read his therapy homework. In short, you make Sherlock Holmes look like an amateur.

Guess what happens? You catch him. He trips up and says something different than what he said before. Or you find out a new detail when you read his therapy homework. Or he sends a sketchy text and you see it. Some new bit of information comes out. Often, it's a small bit, only one little piece of the puzzle, but it's a new bit nonetheless.

From there, the two of you have days of fighting and crying and talking. You do more digging, grilling him about what he has already told you, trying to get to the bottom of this new information plus whatever else you can unearth. To placate you, he tells you a little bit more but certainly not everything – just what he thinks you need to know to get this round of fighting, crying, and talking to settle down so the two of you can get back to normal-ish.

Eventually, things do calm down. You've got another piece or two of the puzzle, and he is swearing once again that you now have the whole story. You are at an impasse, and things settle into an uneasy peace.

Until you once again find out some new detail. Back you go into the vortex of betrayal, feeling once again the waves of shock and pain at being lied to and betrayed, until, worn out with trying to get the truth, you hit the pause button and things settle down yet again. For a while.

This is death by papercut. It is the damaging cycle of repeated rounds of betrayal as the partial truth is trickled out in dribs and drabs. It deepens your mistrust, heightens your trauma symptoms, destroys any goodwill left in the relationship, and maximizes your pain. Worst of all, at the end of all the drama, you still don't have the whole truth.

But what, you ask, is the alternative? You need to know what happened, you have a right to know what happened, and this is the only way you're going to find out, right?

Well, no. There is another option available, and it is to wait until your cheating partner has gotten himself to a place where he is willing and able to tell you the whole truth. And yes, I know that at this stage of the game the very last thing you want to hear is that you are going to have to wait to get the whole story. In fact, the idea that after being lied to, cheated on, manipulated, shamed, and heartbroken, you must wait on the truth until your lying, cheating partner is ready to tell it probably makes you want to throw this book across the room.

I don't blame you. This is so unfair that it's hard to even grasp. The person who mauled your emotions, broke intimate promises, put your health at risk, and stomped on your heart now needs to be treated like some delicate flower who needs... what? Time? Handholding? Help?

You. Must. Be. Joking.

I wish I were. This waiting is actually one of the worst things that betrayed partners must deal with. It feels unfair and postpones the ability to restore some sense of safety in your life. The only thing that brings most betrayed partners in off the ledge during this 'wait it out' phase is recognizing that the alternative – staggered discovery, death by papercut, repeated rounds of betrayal – is even worse and causes you more harm.

Protecting Your Heart

You deserve to know how your relationship agreements have been broken by your cheating partner. You have a right to information about the scope and depth of the betrayal, and you have a right to that information sooner rather than later. The fact that your partner is not yet able/willing to tell the whole truth because his primary allegiance has not yet shifted from protecting his secrets to saving the relationship can leave you feeling helpless and powerless about how to get your needs met.

One of the most important things you can do during this period is to shift out of powerlessness into the empowered action of actively protecting your heart from further trauma. When your partner is still protecting his secrets, he is unfortunately not putting you and your well-being first. As a result, the harm of betrayal continues. New cuts and wounds are added to an already hemorrhaging relationship through the death by papercut cycle I described above. When you stay in a place of trying to get the truth from your cheating partner through some action of your own, you leave yourself open to more lies, more manipulation, and more betrayal.

To move out of this powerlessness trap, you must take a proactive stance to protect your heart and set boundaries around receiving full disclosure.

Disclosure is a facilitated, carefully prepared and supported process where your unfaithful partner provides you with a fully honest account of his history of cheating behaviors. It is a complete accounting, revealing all the behaviors and all the secrets so a new foundation of truth and trust can be established.

To protect your heart and to facilitate the possibility of healing in the relationship, you need disclosure, not more rounds of half-truths and trickled-out information. To protect your heart, you must make a clear request and set a clear boundary around your expectation that your partner will provide you with a full and honest disclosure. Then you will need to give him time and space to work through whatever is blocking his ability to provide that disclosure.

Here is an example of what this might look like. You might say to your partner, "I know that there is information that I do not know about your cheating behaviors. I have a right to know all of what has happened in our relationship and how our relationship agreements have been broken. I need this information to be able to take care of myself appropriately and to determine whether I can move forward in our relationship. I also need to know that you are willing to be completely honest with me and that there will be no more lying and secrets going forward. I need to receive full disclosure from you about the cheating with the help of our therapists. I need this within the next three months. Can you commit to working with your therapist to provide this to me?"

Now, the thought of waiting three months for disclosure may

cause you some heartburn, especially because you may feel like your emotional life is on hold until you fully understand the scope of what has happened. That said, I would encourage you to put a reasonable time limit forward in your request (a minimum of six weeks), and here is why. Most cheaters, when confronted with a request for full disclosure, must work through the fears they have about telling the truth while also working on their habitual patterns of self-deception and lying to others. This work takes time. In addition, once they have accepted responsibility for their actions and committed to providing full disclosure, they need to actually write down the full account of their behaviors. If your partner is dealing with sexual addiction and has a lengthy history of lying and cheating, this too can take a fair amount of time.

If your cheating partner has a skilled therapist, the process of writing the disclosure document may be used to intervene on the behaviors and to help your partner gain insight into who he is and how he arrived in the current situation. These interventions and insights can be helpful to you as well as your partner, as you may begin to see him take more responsibility for his behaviors, extend more empathy and understanding to you, and shift his primary motivation to saving the relationship by being honest and accountable. This process also takes time.

Making a request for full disclosure with a time limit for performance is part one of empowering yourself to protect your heart. Part two is setting boundaries around this request. Boundaries are always about your behavior, not that of another person, because you can't ever control another person's actions or decisions. To determine the boundaries that are appropriate for you, you will need to find some quiet space and ask yourself the following question: "If my partner is unwilling to provide me with full disclosure, what will that mean for me and for my relationship, and what will I then need in order to feel safe?"

This is a painful question to confront. Your hope is that your partner will understand the importance of full honesty and be willing to do the required work to provide you with that. Sadly, not all cheaters are willing to do this, and it is important that you know what steps you need to take in that instance.

Disclosure-related boundaries are different for everyone. Here are some boundaries I have seen betrayed partners create around disclosure. Typically, these boundaries are best stated to the cheating partner in the following way: "If you are not willing to provide full disclosure within the next three months and to be fully and completely honest with me, I will need to..."

- Ask for a therapeutic separation where we live in separate parts of the house or separate residences.
- Ask you to move out of our bedroom.
- Seek legal counsel and file for divorce.
- Ask you to go to inpatient residential treatment.

Whatever boundaries you create, you need to make sure you can and will follow through on them. So, they need to be the right boundaries for you and your circumstances. A skilled therapist can help you come up with the appropriate boundaries for you and your situation. For most partners, receiving full disclosure is a make it or break it issue. Without it, forward movement in the relationship is blocked, as there is no safety without trust and there is no trust without truth.

The last set of disclosure-related boundaries that you will want to create are the boundaries you will implement to protect your heart from further damage while you wait on your partner to prepare his disclosure. These are boundaries that you put in place to stop you from returning to the toxic death by papercut dance of trying to get more information from your partner. These boundaries keep you safe from further harm and increased trauma. These protective boundaries often look like the following:

- I will quit asking for more details and information, and I will wait for you to give me the whole truth in your disclosure.
- I will not try to find your disclosure document or read it

ahead of time when it is only partially written and incomplete. Instead, I will wait to hear you read the entire document to me in an environment where I am supported and you are accountable.

- Until we complete the disclosure process, I will not be sexual with you, as I do not feel safe enough in our relationship to make love without knowing what has happened.
- Until we complete disclosure and for a period after I will only be sexual with you if you use condoms, as I do not yet know the full extent of your behaviors and I must protect my sexual and physical health.
- Until we complete disclosure, I would like a therapeutic separation, as I cannot continue living 'as usual' in our relationship without knowing the full extent of what has happened.

These are just a few examples of boundaries you might implement to protect your heart while you wait for disclosure. Each person is different, and what you need will be different from what another betrayed partner needs. Allow yourself to be in your unique circumstance and to establish the boundaries that are right for you.

One More Step

This chapter may have been particularly triggering to read, and you may have experienced a lot of emotions. If so, that is normal. The issue of being lied to and then trying to get the truth about what has happened is emotionally fraught and filled with anxiety for most people. And waiting on full disclosure is one of the most difficult parts of the healing process for betrayed partners, who often feel unable to heal without full knowledge of the degree of betrayal that has occurred.

If you feel caught in a bind because your cheating partner is still lying to you despite your demands for the truth and clear evidence of how destructive his lying is, do not give up. Go back to the chapter on getting help and look around in your area for a therapist who is trained in facilitating disclosures. Go see this person and enlist his or her help and support in shifting you and your partner out of the death by papercut cycle. If your partner refuses to go with you, go by yourself and get help and support managing his resistance and identifying the choices and boundaries you need in the face of his refusal to become honest or to stop cheating.

Remember, your cheating partner does not have the power to control you or to stop you from healing. You may have to embark on the healing journey by yourself, but you can still move forward out of the confusion and into clarity, freedom, and hope.

9

TO DO: ALLOW THE MOMENT OF TRUTH TO HAPPEN

H ave you caught yourself, even months after the discovery of betrayal, snooping and spying and checking on your cheating partner? If so, here are some common behaviors that you might have engaged in:

- Monitoring computer/phone use through hidden software/apps, keystroke trackers, browser histories, etc.
- Checking wallets, briefcases, pockets, car trunks, gym lockers, etc.
- Obsessively calling or texting your significant other throughout the day to check on where he is and what he is doing.
- Monitoring your partner's location through phone trackers, car trackers, etc.
- Eavesdropping on your partner's phone conversations.
- Monitoring recovery activities such as 12-step meetings, calls to a sponsor, group therapy, individual therapy, completion of homework assignments, etc.
- Searching for and reading your partner's therapy/recovery homework.

For a period after discovery, most partners feel the need for a high level of transparency from the cheating partner regarding his phone/internet use, general whereabouts, and commitment to recovery. Agreements to be fully accountable about these things can help to move a couple out of acute crisis, and to begin the process of rebuilding trust in the relationship.

However, during this time, it can feel like your hyper-vigilance and the knowledge that you are constantly checking on things is what keeps your cheating partner on the straight and narrow. And there may be some truth to this. At the very least, it lets your cheating partner know that you are serious about things changing for the better in lasting ways if you are to remain in the relationship (as opposed to just changing for a while and then going back).

At some point, however, you must allow what I call 'the moment of truth' to happen in your relationship. The moment of truth is when you step out of immediate crisis management mode and look at the big picture of what you want and need in your relationship.

Immediately after discovery, you need the emotional hemorrhaging to stop. You need to know that no more cheating is occurring and the lying has ceased. But long-term you need much more than this. You need to know that your cheating partner is doing whatever it takes to ensure that he will never again betray you or lie to you as he has done in the past. You also need to know that your trust is based on the vigilance of your significant other, who is consistently practicing new thinking, attitudes, and behaviors that will ensure that he is sober sexually and emotionally. Trust should not be based on your constant monitoring and hyper-awareness.

What you long for is to know that your cheating partner has truly changed and is not going to betray or hurt you again. You want to be able to relax in the relationship, to let down your guard and feel safe about trusting your partner. You want to know that whether your cheating partner is home alone for a weekend, on a business trip to the Philippines, or in the basement paying bills at ten o'clock at night, he has the tools, ability, and commitment to stay sober and faithful to you and your relationship agreements.

The problem with staying in Sherlock Holmes mode is that you prevent yourself from ever finding out if this is possible in your relationship. If you continue to be the most significant form of energy pushing for fidelity and recovery, you block your partner's and your own ability to find out if he is ever going to become truly trustworthy again. To avoid this stagnation, you must allow the moment of truth to occur.

The moment of truth is when you shift your energy away from monitoring and checking on your cheating partner. When you stop monitoring and checking his activities, it creates an opportunity for you to see if he is truly committed to recovery and repairing the relationship. It creates space for you to find out if, when you are no longer the energy behind recovery, your partner stays the course.

This is a big risk. What if, when you let down your guard, your significant other stops pursuing recovery or starts cheating again? What if the moment of truth reveals a reality that you don't think you can handle or want to face? Sadly, this is a possible outcome.

However, the opposite can also happen. You can find out that when you shift your energy away from mistrust, your significant other maintains his focus and energy toward recovery and healing the relationship. You can find out that trust is being rebuilt – trust that does not require hyper-vigilance on your part but instead creates a path toward true connection and safety in the relationship.

Risking the moment of truth is scary. There can be enormous rewards. There can be heartbreaking disappointments. Either way, avoiding the moment of truth leaves you stuck in a never-ending cycle of active trauma symptoms and prevents your long-term healing.

Your Cheating Partner's Moment of Truth

Two things motivate change in human beings: fear and desire. After the crisis of betrayal, fear is what initially motivates and drives the process of change. However, to achieve long-term transformation, a person's motivation must eventually shift from fear to desire.

In the beginning, your cheating partner's recovery is usually driven by fear – mostly fear of losing the relationship. He enters recovery not because he wants to change his behavior and make amends, but because he does not want to lose his relationship with you. Going to therapy, attending group and 12-step meetings, doing homework, making phone calls to supportive peers and mentors, and changing long-ingrained habits are all motivated, at least initially, by fear of losing the relationship.

You, as the betrayed partner, are also motivated by fear – fear that you will be hurt again, fear that if you don't stay on top of the cheater he will do it again, fear that he won't be willing to do what is necessary to heal your relationship. So, the crisis of betrayal trauma creates massive fear for you and your partner alike, as your relationship is brought to the brink of destruction. This fear pushes both of you to work toward change.

However, as I've already said, there is a moment in the recovery journey when you as the betrayed partner need to step back and allow your cheating partner's energy, rather than your pain and his fear of losing the relationship, to become the primary motivating force. What this means is that the moment of truth is as important for your cheating partner as it is for you and your relationship. This is the moment when he must move beyond the pain and fear-driven paradigm of early recovery and find within himself a different impetus for change and healing.

This means your partner must connect with what he wants for himself long-term. What does he want his relationship to look like? What will a healthy sex life look like? What does he want for his children? What does he want for his friendships? What is his value system? What does it mean for him to live a congruent life where his values and his behaviors are in alignment? Who does he want to be?

Connecting to these deep desires about relationships, meaning, purpose, and legacy is a key task in your partner's recovery process. Often, infidelity and addiction hijack a cheater's life, pushing him off course and diverting his energy and attention away from what he truly believes in and values. Rediscovering and connecting to his truest, deepest desires and beliefs about what gives life meaning and purpose transforms his motivation for recovery, shifting him away from pain and fear and connecting him to his true longings and desires for the future.

Fear-based motivation takes an enormous toll on the goodwill in the relationship, as it requires both the cheater and the betrayed partner to stay in constant connection with the pain, fear, and damage that infidelity has brought. Couples who are unable to move out of the pain/fear phase of recovery and into the longing/desire phase often find themselves stuck in a toxic relational cycle. This can only be sustained for so long. Thus, the transition from fear-based motivation to desire-based motivation is vital to long-term recovery and healing.

For your cheating partner to make the transition from fear-based to desire-based motivation, he must quit looking to you as the primary driver of his recovery. He must quit using your pain as the energy behind the changes he is making. He must find his own reasons for changing. He must connect to his own desires, his own vision for life and relationship, and his own longing for things to be different. These must become the primary motivators that energize him and sustain him for the long-term.

If you haven't risked the moment of truth yet, consider having a discussion with your cheating partner about the need for the two of you, as a couple, to make this transition. Take this topic into couple's therapy and get assistance with it there. And know that making this transition is not a one-time deal. You will loop back into the fear at times, but you will come out of it quicker and find your footing faster if you and your partner are focused on the long-term vision of what you long for and want for yourselves and your relationship.

WHAT NOT TO DO: AVOID THE MOMENT OF TRUTH

As discussed above, it is important that eventually the primary energy behind recovery and repair of the relationship comes from your cheating partner, not from you. This means you must allow a moment of truth to occur, where you stop monitoring and checking your partner's behaviors and regularly reminding him of what he has done.

When you do this in your relationship, you may find that your partner is committed to his recovery, and that he continues to work on himself and the relationship not to appease you, but because he wants to take responsibility for what he has done and to heal the relationship. He may even find that he's committed to change and recovery for himself regardless of whether the relationship with you works out. You may see him building relationships with other men and allowing them to hold him accountable while they speak truth into his life. Best of all, you may discover that you can begin to trust him and to relax because he and his support system are 'manning the wall' and being vigilant to ensure that he does not return to his old patterns.

This, of course, is what most betrayed partners hope they will see. It is the foundation on which real healing can take place both individually and within the relationship.

However, when you allow the moment of truth to occur, you run the risk of a quite different outcome. You may find that when you lower your guard and stop your monitoring behaviors that your cheating partner slacks off. New behaviors revert to old behaviors. Maybe he quits going to 12-step meetings, cancels therapy appointments, misses group, isn't on the phone to his sponsor or others in his support system, relaxes boundaries that he has told you he needs, and abandons some of the healthy new habits he has created. You may find that suddenly you are having the same weird conversations you used to have with him. You may realize that you are being manipulated and lied to again. You may find that your cheating partner has been 'doing recovery' to appease you, and not because he is committed to long-term change for himself and the relationship.

This is a scary, heartbreaking thing to find out.

And because the moment of truth is so risky, you might avoid this moment. This avoidance is usually unconscious. You don't even realize you are doing it. The part of you that seeks safety and wants to minimize threats to yourself and your relationship unconsciously avoids the moment of truth because that moment risks more pain and disappointment.

A primary way to avoid the moment of truth is to never let your guard down to see if, when you stop being the primary energy pushing for change, your cheating partner maintains (or even raises) his energy and effort level and takes responsibility for changing himself and repairing the relationship. Instead of risking further betrayal, you continue monitoring, checking up, reminding, asking, probing, and reminding yet again.

Behind these behaviors is fear – fear of finding out that your cheating partner won't do what needs to be done to repair the damage. And underneath this first layer of fear is the deeper fear that you are not worth it to your partner, that you don't matter enough to him, that his refusal to do the work and take responsibility is about him not caring enough about you, your family, and your relationship.

Rather than find out what is true in your relationship, you avoid the truth because it has the potential to break your heart all over again.

However, by avoiding the moment of truth you handicap yourself and your relationship. You limit yourself because you keep yourself stuck in the belief that it is your trauma symptoms (hyper-vigilance is a trauma symptom) that keep your cheating partner in recovery. If this is true, then you can't allow your trauma symptoms to heal. You and your cheating partner must continue to experience your trauma symptoms so that he will stay the course.

This may sound absurd at first. Most partners are consciously trying to reduce their trauma symptoms and feel better. But what I have observed both in myself when I was going through the process and in the countless betrayed partners I have treated is that unconsciously, because of the fear of further betrayal, we believe it is our trauma symptoms that keep our partner from betraying us again. The changes in our behavior – our pain and distress and hyper-vigilance – provide a constant reminder to him of what he has done so that he will not forget and backslide into old patterns.

This fear can create a cyclical dynamic for betrayed partners. You begin to feel a little better, maybe for a few hours or a few days, and that is a welcome relief. But this relief brings with it the fearful suspicion that if you feel better and are not in acute distress, your cheating partner will forget, or become complacent, or go straight back to his cheating behaviors. Instead of the relief cueing safety, it cues danger. When this happens, the progress toward stabilization and healing is interrupted. Instead of progressing, you find that your mind turns toward and becomes preoccupied with past hurts and the possibility of future pain.

This happens involuntarily for the most part. Our threat systems begin to sense danger if we allow ourselves to relax in the presence of someone who has hurt us. What if they hurt us again? Our defensive/protective system reminds us of the betrayal by bringing us back to our pain and distress. Suddenly, we find ourselves re-running mind movies about the cheating, re-reading hurtful texts between our significant other and his acting out partners, and asking about details and information we have already asked about and had answered several times. All these behaviors are a result of our threat system trying to help us avoid more danger by staying vigilant and prepared. However, the result is that they bring us back into the pain and distress of the original betrayal and reactivate our trauma symptoms.

Let me repeat what I said earlier. Usually, this cycle is based on an unconscious belief that it is your trauma symptoms – your pain, distress, sadness, and anger – that keep your cheating partner from hurting you again. And if this is true, then you can't allow your trauma symptoms to heal. You and your cheating partner must continue to experience your trauma symptoms so he will stay committed to the recovery process.

This is no way to live long term. For true healing to happen, the moment of truth must be risked. You must be willing to stop having your pain be the primary motivator for your cheating partner's engagement in the healing process. Taking the risk, while scary, is what sets you free – free to make the very best decisions for yourself, and free to heal, regardless of the outcome for your relationship.

10

TO DO: SHOW YOURSELF KINDNESS

At the end of the day, after all the advice and support I have tried to offer in this book, the biggest best piece of wisdom that I can give you as you deal with betrayal is to be kind to yourself. This may also be the most trite-sounding piece of advice. One that makes you think, 'Yeah yeah yeah, I know I need to do that.' It can almost feel like a burden – one more thing you should be doing that you are not doing well enough. Which, of course, is the last thing I want you to feel. So, let's unpack this together and identify what being kind to yourself in the aftermath of betrayal really looks like, because there are some very concrete things you can do that will help you.

Create Space for Your Feelings

We live in a culture that does not approve of big feelings. We don't approve of little feelings very much either. All the feelings that we have are supposed to be kept neatly tucked out of sight. In fact, men aren't supposed to have feelings at all. And if you are female, you have likely been conditioned to make room for your male partner's feelings and to caretake him while keeping your feelings subdued so as to not overwhelm him.

This cultural expectation, that when you experience grievous losses and hurts you will keep your pain, anger, and sadness to yourself, is a recipe for addiction, mental illness, and physical health problems. It is like holding a beach ball under the water. The deeper you push it under, the more forcefully it will eventually burst up and out, flying off in random directions.

This is true in all facets of life, including sexual betrayal. When you experience this or any other type of betrayal, you automatically enter a grieving process. You experience an enormous sense of loss. The loss of the person you thought you were in a relationship with. The loss of your relationship history as you once knew it. The loss of your unsullied dreams for the future. Last but not least, the loss of your sense of self as your body is swept up in a powerful trauma response. All of these losses are felt and experienced simultaneously, and you plunge into grief.

And grief is inconvenient. It is its own master. It shows up when and how it wants. You can be in a grocery store, minding your own business, and a random stranger does or says something that reminds you of your situation. In a singular moment, you can go from fine to furious, calm to panic, clarity to confusion, collected to falling apart. Without warning, these waves of feeling can overtake you, flooding your senses and clamoring for release.

During times in my life when I have experienced significant grief, one of the things that always shocks me is the way that life keeps on going. I remember when my good friend Jason died a few years ago. I loved Jason. He was one of my favorite people, a bigger than life personality, an extraordinarily gifted artist, and he died in his late-30s from a cancer that mowed him down in less than three months.

When he died, I experienced several days of intense grief before things settled down into a more subdued form of sadness. During the initial intense feelings of loss, life felt surreal and confusing. How was it that Jason was gone and I still had to go to work, still had to interact with people who had no idea what I was feeling inside, still had to cook dinner and brush my teeth and do all the mundane chores that make up daily living? It seemed odd and confusing that life could just keep on going when something so momentous and horrifying and unfair had just happened. I felt like I needed a moment when everything would just stop and there would be a universal pause to acknowledge the loss that the world had just sustained.

But that did not happen. And it does not happen and will not happen for you, either. Your boss will still expect you to perform admirably at work. Your children will still be fussy and difficult at times. Your schedule will still be full, and you will feel obligated to show up and smile despite a heart full of dread and pain.

Without the cultural support and approval to grieve your losses publicly and in community, you may find yourself trying to figure out what to do when you are in the middle of the grocery store and suddenly you really need to ugly cry.

So here is what you do. You leave your cart. You just leave it. No one cares. You go out to your car, and you move your car if you can to an empty corner of the parking lot, and you cry. You ugly cry until you get it all out. You snot and heave and bawl until all the feelings that got triggered in the grocery store have moved through you and you are calm and spent.

This is not likely to be convenient, as most of us are on a schedule most of the time. This may make you late or make you miss something altogether. You may end up feeling like you do a lot of apologizing for a period as you give yourself space and permission to process the grief and loss that keeps surfacing.

However, I cannot tell you how important it is that you give yourself permission to feel your feelings and allow them to move through you. Doing this allows your body to move all the way through the stress response cycle triggered by the person in the grocery store. Without this, you will continue to push the beach ball deeper under water until you can hold it no more and it careens up and out whether you want it to or not.

When you are triggered, your body's threat response system fires and feelings of fear, panic, rage, and anger rush through you. If you do not allow these feelings to be felt, they will stay inside you, replaying in an endless loop of traumatic response. And this can leave you susceptible to using unhealthy coping mechanisms (drinking, being inappropriately sexual, overeating, etc.) to suppress and manage your feelings.

It Is far better to give yourself permission to feel the feelings and allow them to move through and out of your body. You can do this in all kinds of ways. You can cry, you can scream, you can say a mantra, you can journal, you can run, walk, bike, or swim. You can play with your pet, you can talk to a friend, you can connect with your partner (if helpful). You can pray, you can go out and spend time in nature, you can take a bath.

This is where self-care and self-kindness come in. It is an act of profound kindness, tenderness, and self-care to give yourself some space and time to feel your feelings. So give yourself whatever you need in the moment that will help your feelings of grief move through you. When you give yourself this kindness, you will feel the release and relief that comes when your distress is tended and released with love and care.

Validate Your Feelings

We are not quite done with the topic of feelings. There is one more big kindness that you can show yourself around your feelings, and when you do it, it will make a world of difference in how you feel. This simple act of kindness is to actively validate your feelings.

This, of course, is easier said than done for most of us. In fact, I hear a litany of invalidation all day long as I sit with my clients:

"I shouldn't feel this way, but..."

"I know I need to move on, but..."

"I don't know why I'm still so sad, but..."

"I don't know what's wrong with me, but..."

"I know I shouldn't still be angry, but..."

"I don't know why I'm not over this, but..."

Most of the time, my clients have no idea that they are invalidating their feelings. They are so used to doing it, so culturally brain-washed to believe that big feelings are an indicator that something is wrong with them, that the language of invalidation is unconsciously woven into their speech. The invalidation is spoken without their awareness.

Unfortunately, when we invalidate our feelings in this way, we increase our stress, thereby reinforcing the threat response in our bodies and putting ourselves at war with the natural processes of grief and loss that are trying to heal us. We keep ourselves stuck.

If instead you greet your feelings with kindness, tenderness, and a validating spirit, an opening is created. There is suddenly space for those feelings to be felt, to be believed (because even though feelings are not facts they are information), and to be released.

Years ago, I was trained by Pia Mellody in her developmental trauma model. Pia has a wonderful phrase that she uses to describe what happens when we invalidate our feelings:

Explosive episodes of reality surfacing.

When we invalidate our feelings and tamp them down, we set ourselves up for an explosion. Instead of feeling our anger when it comes up and validating our anger by saying, "I am angry about _____, and I have a right to be angry," we push it down and tell ourselves we should be over it by now. When we do this, the anger piles on top of other anger and begins to fester into resentment. So, piled on top of the anger we now have a layer of resentment from the belief that we aren't supposed to be angry. Eventually, of course, our anger and resentment will surface, often as rage. Or, as Pia Mellody says, we have explosive episodes of reality surfacing.

When I am training therapists who are learning to work with betrayal trauma, they often tell me stories of 'explosive episodes of reality surfacing' with their clients. Breakables are thrown, the police are called, the neighbors can hear the shouting. I listen and nod and then say, "Yes, your client is having trouble feeling her anger." When I say this, I usually get a pause, a blink or two of the eyes, and then a frown. The therapist will say, "No, I think she's quite connected to her anger. I don't think that's what's going on."

And I will say, "No, she is having rage because she feels conflicted about her anger. Her anger is being suppressed and is also mixing with her shame, pain, sadness, powerlessness, and fear. And then it's all surfacing as rage. You need to help her connect to and validate her anger as she feels it so she can express it from her most authentic self. She will come out of her rage only when she has permission to feel and express her anger freely and from her heart. Your job is to help her do that."

This is true not just with anger. All our feelings need to be validated, especially in the aftermath of betrayal when emotions become a hodge-podge that makes no rational sense. If you feel drawn to your partner and want to make love with him, validate that feeling. Have safe sex and allow yourself to know that being drawn to someone who has betrayed you but is also the love of your life is normal and understandable. If you want nothing to do with your partner and want him to go away and give you space, validate those feelings. Your anger and pain are asking for time and room to be felt. Give yourself that. If you feel confused and uncertain, tell yourself, "Of course I feel this way, my world has just been turned upside down," and allow those feelings to be real and present. If you feel sad, cry. If you feel lonely, reach out. If you feel shame, tell someone who loves you. If you feel pain, seek comfort. If you feel anger, speak it from your heart. If you feel love, share it.

Whatever you feel, meet that feeling with curiosity about what it is telling you, and allow it to be present. As I said earlier, feelings are not facts, and you don't need to do anything with them other than letting them be present. But doing this very simple thing – validating your feelings – will change your life in powerful ways.

WHAT NOT TO DO: EXPECT TOO MUCH FROM YOURSELF

In the aftermath of betrayal, your body and mind are struggling with an ongoing trauma response. As we have discussed, betrayal is something that unfolds over time, and your understanding of your altered reality, what it means for you, and what happens next will unfold over time as well.

This means that for some weeks and months, you are not going to be functioning the way you did before learning about the betrayal. Your energy is going to be different (probably lower); your body may have symptoms (illness, headaches, stomach problems, twitching eyes or limbs); your mind will likely be scattered, and your ability to concentrate, focus, and track information will be impaired.

This can be disorienting. Not only have you lost the relationship you thought you had with your partner, you have lost yourself. Who you were and the parts of yourself that you depended on seem to have gone missing. Instead of the competent, organized, dependable person you are used to being, you are suddenly disorganized, forgetful, unreliable, confused, and uncertain.

One of the important things to remember when experiencing these types of trauma symptoms is that they are *temporary*. They may last weeks or even months, but they will eventually subside and you will return to your usual self. Your disorientation is not a permanent state of being, and it is important to remind yourself of that. Otherwise, you may start to worry that you will never feel normal again. But you will. It is just a matter of time.

The biggest kindness that you can give yourself during this period is patience and realistic expectations. You are not going to be able to do the same number of things you were doing before. You are not going to be able to do those things as well as before. You are not going to be able to tolerate the same levels of normal daily stress (stress from juggling your job, kids, house, husband, etc.) You are going to expend enormous amounts of energy and emotional resources processing the betrayal, and that will inevitably affect you in significant ways. You will not have a lot of focus and energy left over for a while, and life will need to change so you can give yourself the space and time you need to heal.

This means that you will need to learn the word "no." No, I cannot take on an extra day of driving carpool. No, I cannot bring cookies to the classroom for that event. No, I cannot take on an extra project right now. No, I cannot have your parents come to visit this weekend. No, I cannot meet that deadline. No, I cannot volunteer for that position. No, I cannot read you one more story tonight. No, I cannot make love right now. No, I cannot cook dinner this evening. No, I cannot run that errand for you.

That said, you are going to have to keep functioning. Very few of us can go to bed for two months, two weeks, or even two days without creating issues in our lives – even when we're dealing with a crisis. You are not likely to be an exception. Rather, you are a grown-up, and that means you have responsibilities and obligations that cannot be ignored. Adulting is hard work all the time, doubly so after a trauma.

So, if you can't crawl in bed for two weeks but I'm suggesting you learn to say no, how do you find the balance? The balance is found in accepting that life is going to need to change for a while. Anything extra that can be taken off your plate should be taken off. To this end, you need to think about what is essential for you to do and what is extra that you can say no to. And you are going to want to check in with yourself regularly each day to see how you are doing and what your energy level is, adjusting your expectations accordingly.

This may mean that your family eats more takeout that you would typically care to feed them so you can go to work and function while still managing to get your kids where they need to be on time. You just might not have the energy at the end of the day to also cook a meal, and that is perfectly OK. Nobody is going to die from eating takeout for a few weeks. Rather than pressuring yourself to do what you used to do, you need to extend kindness, grace, and patience to yourself and know that everyone will be alright while you work through the crisis you are in.

Being kind to yourself in this way might also mean that invitations from friends and family are more selectively responded to as you determine what you can and can't add to your schedule given your current emotional and energetic resources. It may mean that the extra project you and your boss have been talking about needs to be pushed back a few weeks so you can focus on your regular work duties and responsibilities and keep those in good order while you work through the crisis. It may mean you are more tired, more forget-ful, need more time to get things done, and need more breaks, more naps, and more rest.

So many of my clients expect the same level of performance from themselves despite the crisis they're in, and when they can't meet their expectations they are mean to, judgmental, and critical of them-selves. They would never treat a friend who was going through betrayal that way, but they talk to themselves with a drill-sergeant tone that demands far more than they can realistically give.

One of the biggest kindnesses you can give yourself after betrayal is to set realistic expectations and extend enormous amounts of patience and grace to yourself. While it may seem counterintuitive, doing this will actually help you to heal faster, as you will have the emotional space and time you need to tend to the enormous, life-changing process of healing.

AFTERWORD

If you have just read this book then you likely know exactly what it means to experience your world 'break bad' through betrayal. Most betrayed partners dealing with the shock of discovering cheating are trying to figure out what has happened and what actions they should take in response.

I hope that this book has given you some answers to those questions and provided you with direction and guidance about how to move forward. Not everything you have just read will apply to you immediately. Understanding how betrayal has impacted you and healing from it is an unfolding process and each stage has its own particular issues, questions and emotions. Allow yourself to be where you are and know that this resource is available for you to return to at different times when you need to hear the message from a particular chapter or section again.

And, as always, be kind to yourself and know that you are not alone, many others are journeying with you and supporting you as you heal.

PASS IT ON

If this book has been helpful for you (and I hope it has!) one way you can help it reach more betrayed partners is to give it a positive review on Amazon. Amazon prioritizes books based on the number of reviews the book gets, so having reviews helps more people be able to find the book and read it. To post a review please go to: http://bit.ly/BreaksBad

ABOUT THE AUTHOR

Michelle D. Mays LPC, CSAT-S is the founder of PartnerHope, a comprehensive resource and online community offering authentic hope and practical help to individuals and couples recovering from Betrayal Trauma.

She is also the founder and Clinical Director of the Center for Relational Recovery, serving individuals and couples struggling with sexual addiction, betrayal trauma, childhood trauma, and relationship issues.

Michelle is a Certified Sex Addiction Therapist and Supervisor trained under Dr. Patrick Carnes. She is also trained in Post Induction Therapy (for the treatment of relational trauma) by Pia Mellody. She is currently completing her certification in Emotionally Focused Therapy for couples. She is a Registered Supervisor with the state of Virginia and is licensed as a Professional Counselor in both Virginia and Washington DC.

On a personal note, here are a few things to know about Michelle. Snow makes her happy. Reading is her favorite. She hates asparagus. The beach is the happiest place on earth. Her siblings and sibling-in-laws make her laugh out loud. She regularly refers to her dog as "her lab-ness." She would rather not be bored. Ever. A night out with friends can't be beat. Music makes life worth living. Interior design is her secret fixation and she wants to come back as Joanna Gaines in her next life. A morning spent writing on her sun porch is the best morning ever. A tent and a campfire almost always end in tears (usually from laughter but sometimes not). And she *really* wishes she could teleport.

facebook.com/partnerhope

twitter.com/partnerhope

MORE HOPE AND HELP

For more hope and help in recovering from Betrayal Trauma visit PartnerHope.com.

ALSO BY MICHELLE D. MAYS, LPC, CSAT-S

The Aftermath of Betrayal

Betrayal Trauma Crisis and Risk Assessment Tool (Available for free
download at www.PartnerHope.com)

Made in the USA
Las Vegas, NV
24 November 2024

12527695R00066